MASSIVE CAREER SUCCESS

How to Create the Life of Your Dreams!

MOJIBUR DOFTORI, PhD

POWERHOUSE
— PUBLICATIONS —

Powerhouse Publications
Suite 124. 94 London Road
Oxford, OX3 9FN UNITED KINGDOM

www.powerhousepublishing.com

To my wife, Syeda Tutu

CONTENTS

INTRODUCTION

You too can achieve massive career success. It's in your own hands. You may ask: why do millions of people in this world fail to fulfill their career potential? Why do they live less productive, average, frustrated, unhappy and miserable lives? Poor self-understanding, misplaced focus, lack of goal setting, lethargy and, most importantly, lack of action are some of the key reasons why people fail to achieve career success. If they take on a task, they rarely complete it. Instead of proactively pursing a worthy goal, they spend time in idle socializing, gossiping and reacting to circumstances. They become complainers. They suffer from jealousy, shame, guilt and fear. They fail to understand that success is a matter of positive mindset and a way of effective living.

If you possess the right mindset, financial, or other constraints, cannot hold you back from realizing your dream. This is an inner process that builds on personal development, creating inner resources and making yourself valuable in the marketplace. While pursuing material gain in life is important, becoming a person of vision, values and skills is far more essential. The latter can add tremendous value not only in career advancement but also improve your significance in family and society. It will distinguish you from the crowd. The bottom line is this: you must act responsibly in order to boost your career.

Broadly speaking, everybody wishes to be successful in their career. But most traditional, certificate-based education fails to instill useful and specialized skills for career success. It creates elevation of diplomas only. As a result, higher education is not a guarantee for career success any more. In order to keep yourself relevant in the changing job market, you must develop useful knowledge, skills and experience. When you are able to combine imagination and true passion with disciplined action, miracles take place. Career success is a self-directed personal process to create your own value in the marketplace. It's less about competition with others and more about being skillful and resourceful. If you reach this state, you experience a true adventure of the mind. Imagine how a caterpillar transforms from its cocoon into a butterfly that takes flight, and drinks nectar from the flowers, in its very short life cycle. To attain such joy, you must go through a painful transformation. Remember, there are no free meals in this world. Every success has a price tag on it. No pain, no gain. You must make yourself valuable in the marketplace in order to achieve massive career success. To reach this goal, you must discover your special gifts or talents in life and nurture those.

Unfortunately, the vast majority of people fail to discover their gifts, let alone nurture them. Instead of crafting a personalized career plan and going beyond their comfort zone, they blindly copy others. Without any clear purpose and mission in life, they simply react to circumstances. Instead of changing themselves, they want to change the world first. This is indeed unrealistic. It's a surefire way to end up living a life of frustration, unhappiness, misery and resentment. In this mindset, people wrongly consider career success as a "zero-sum" game — i.e. one person's gain is another's loss. In fact, success in this world is not in short supply. You can be as successful as you want to be. There is no limit to it. But first, you must get your mindset right. Getting a sense of self-understanding, self-acceptance and taking ownership of your life are crucial in this regard. To change the world, you have to change yourself first. Otherwise, you will end up in the same state as the Indian parable of the blind men who chanced upon an elephant for the first time. By touching one part of the gigantic animal's body, each of them got only a partial understanding of it. Without getting a broader view of the animal, they each guessed its shape based on their own partial understanding, and then argued with others.

For career success, you must have a clear understanding of the nature, purpose, potential and limitations of human life. It's about getting clarity on your personality type, as well as your areas of strength and potential. Keeping these in mind and choosing the right career based on your personal value system, you can build up the career of your dreams. By following this path, you can become an effective and dynamic person. You must learn to take risks, to make mistakes and to appear stupid to others. This will separate you from millions of average people who are too afraid to fail. When you claim your individuality, it will make your life exciting and impactful.

You may become famous as a byproduct of your success. While it is true that talents or abilities can be innate, anybody can achieve any skill and fulfill their potential through focused and concentrated action. It is important to underline the fact that any meaningful change in life requires individual actions. You should aim at becoming the best version of yourself rather than only acquiring material wealth. You may lose material wealth such as money, but if you become a person of value and substance, this will remain with you throughout your life. When you become a valuable person in yourself, you will naturally be prosperous.

This book will help you to discover your true gifts and define the purpose of your life; it will give you a proven easy-to-implement formula for your career as well as your life success. It will also provide you with practical tools and techniques to work on yourself. These will increase your professional knowledge and skills as well as making you an effective person. This will unlock your true potential and open up a new world of opportunities. It will help in preparing you to withstand career shocks emanating from the adoption of artificial intelligence and automation in the workplace. It doesn't matter whether you are a teenager or in your seventies – age should not be a barrier to your success. At any age, you can build up a brand new career or take your existing career to a new height. It's never too early or too late. You don't need to wait to reach for an ideal moment. In fact, you can start today from where you are right now. Remember that success is not a destination. It's a journey. For success, you must keep going.

This book provides examples of the world's most successful people from various fields. It also draws examples from ordinary people who transformed their lives, became massively successful and made the world a better place through their indomitable spirit.

You can adapt and adopt their lessons in your career development so that, whatever walk of life you are in, you can achieve phenomenal success. By using the easy-to-follow self-assessment checklist at the end of each chapter, you will be able to craft a career plan that suits your personal strengths, needs and circumstances. This book provides rare time-tested truths, lessons and wisdom that you may profitably use to put your life in perspective. Millions of people throughout the world don't have access to such valuable life lessons. This book sheds light on how to develop new habits – the key ingredient of building skills and competence for making career breakthroughs.

Whether you are a beginner or an expert in any field, you will find this book highly valuable. It will provide you with useful tips, tools and techniques for massive career success. It will remove many dysfunctional myths from your mind about success. It will give you clarity on what exactly you need to become successful. It will motivate you to take concrete action for success. By following the guidelines in this book, you will see career success in a broader perspective. You will be able to create significant value in the marketplace and attract success in life. By following the formula of this book, you will not only be massively successful in your career, but in life in general. Overall, you will be a high performer. The world will open new and larger roles for you. Success will be reflected in all areas of your life.

CHAPTER 1

WHY DO PEOPLE FAIL?

Why do people fail to live up to their true potential? There are a number of factors that hinder people's success. Mindset is the central factor that determines one's success or failure in life. People's primary socialization in family, school and community shapes their imagination and worldview. Negative thoughts, self-doubt, fear of failure, lack of willpower, making of excuses and lack of planned actions create an "average" mindset or the mindset of "failure." This stops people from getting a true understanding of themselves and their purpose of life. As a result, people become passive participants in life. People become doubtful about their capability of leading a life of their own choosing. They irrationally expect that someone else will appear in their life to magically rescue them from their messes. Others will take them to the mythical land of milk and honey. As they don't take charge of their lives, they live their lives based on impulses and resultant frustration, fear and anger. They fail to discover their needs, strengths and true potential. They become slaves to dependent habits. Their fates are dictated by external circumstances over which they have no control. Others have way too much control over their lives. To become successful, you must assert control over your life. You must stop wasting time. It will enable you to build up personal capacities to handle challenges effectively.

In fact, our lives are an accumulated result of the choices we make or fail to make. Imagine a boy who wanted to become a doctor. Suppose he ended up joining the police force instead in order to fulfill his parents' wishes. Alternatively, imagine a boy who wanted to become a police officer yet ended up being a doctor or nurse. The mismatch between one's true passion and actual profession leads people to perform poorly in their work. It is also reflected in poor productivity in their career. Work may turn out to be a punishment or boring duty for them. They may worry more about their appearance to others than improving their skills and doing things with the right focus. This professional mismatch creates work-related mental stress that leads to burnout and lowered productivity. Millions of people across the world suffer from poor motivation and lower productivity in the workplace. Billions of euros are lost to state, society and the markets every year because of this.

We all know that life is never perfect. Your mission in life is therefore to take it from imperfection and move it in the direction of perfection. Pain and change are a natural part of human life. It's not bookish knowledge but experience that makes people truly educated. Many people fail to understand that hardships and challenges are in fact boons in disguise. Used positively, they help to transform lives for the better. Instead of blaming the world, you should try to increase your personal skills and competence to face challenges more effectively. You must use pain to fuel your success. Many people fail to identify their true passion, let alone using it for enhancing their professional development. Their personal talents and strengths remain under-utilized. As they lack inner direction, they fail to initiate change. Many are, in fact, afraid of change. Even though some may earn lots of money through inheritance or luck, this cannot provide them with direction in life. A life lived without an inner compass cannot be an effective life. A person's conflicting values and actions create inner contradictions and psychological mess. This leads people to end up battling against themselves. It is tragic. In this scenario, people may attempt to impress others through pretense and drama. This is a superficial and futile exercise. People without a roadmap to their life can easily get dissuaded by an uncertain, unpredictable or unpleasant experience.

As people grow older, they may get more of a sense of direction, based on their personal experiences. Yet, many fail to take action or ownership of their lives. They may wish to dramatically improve their living conditions and social standing without challenging or changing themselves. They think they are too old for changing their life path. As a result, their desires and dreams remain mere wishes only. Unable to take control of their lives, they fail to attract success. They expect magical solutions to their career, as if they could rub Aladdin's Lamp and have their wishes granted. They may get enticed to become successful by seeing other people's success. They fail to understand that these people are successful because they have done their career planning and acted upon it. As their commitment to action is not purposeful or internally driven, they cannot keep going with action till the end. Their commitment takes the fate of many New Year's resolutions – it dies down in the first two or three weeks of the year due to procrastination. They find the easiest excuses to blame others for their failure. They develop a victim mentality that makes them appear as mere products of chance or luck. This fatalistic viewpoint enables them to hand over their personal power to others. As they possess no clearly-defined purpose or compelling reason to act, their wishes stay as wishes only. They remain poorly motivated. It's no wonder that this happens to millions of people around the world. The vast majority of students, from high school to university, get little or no career guidance in many parts of the world. As a result, the majority of people can find no sense of direction in their life. Below, you will find the main reasons why people fail to live up to their true potential.

GETTING STUCK IN THE PAST

Life does not appear fair to many people. Bad things happen to everyone at one time or another. While good memories of the past inspire us, the bad memories give us pain. Past pain may overshadow people's present, as well as their future. It may make them revengeful. What is the point of thinking about revenge or taking revenge against others? Is it useful? What's the end result? One thing is evident: it consumes valuable energy without any productive contribution to your future. If you take revenge, what's the difference between you and the person who committed the wrong against you? If you carry the intention to take revenge but can't act upon it, it can be poisonous for your mind. In this situation, who wins? Memories of the past are useful as long as they can work as lessons for the present and future. If you cannot use your memories, good or bad, to guide your current actions then they are useless. What's the point of carrying the baggage of negative memories that do not serve you? Better to use this for a productive purpose or drop the baggage altogether.

So, either use your painful memories to fuel success or discard them to make space for good things in your mind. In either case, it will help you to develop and excel yourself. This requires practising self-understanding and mindfulness to others. Buddha teaches us that we suffer because of our own ignorance or limited understanding of ourselves and things around us. In many instances, people have no control over their life. Because of limited self-understanding and understanding of the nature of life in general, people may get frustrated, disoriented and may hurt others. If you happen to be in such a person's way at the wrong time, you may feel the heat of his rage. It's nothing about you. Just any random person may feel his negative outpouring. Imagine a child growing up in the family of such a disoriented parent. The troubled home upbringing may have damaging effects on the child's mind even in their adulthood.

Life may appear full of difficulties. You may become overwhelmed by situations, like a bird that has its tail stuck in thick tar on a roof-top. When it gets its tail unstuck, its beak becomes stuck. When it gets the beak unstuck, its tail gets stuck again. The only way the tarred bird can get out of this sorry state is to take actions based on seeing the bigger picture. If you can see yourself in the broader canvass of life, you can stay calm in a difficult situation and find a way out without being overwhelmed by it. Panicking doesn't help, but understanding the broader picture and finding appropriate strategy do.

We don't judge the people we love. That's why we overlook the shortcomings of our family members and close friends. You need to extend this compassion to others too. It will open up space for new positive experiences in life. You have to remember that you cannot change the past, but you can change your attitude to it. It is imperative that you erase painful memories of the past saying, "never again" and use those to fuel your success. Or even better, take such unpleasant or uncomfortable memories as lessons for the future. What you must do is work on your future now so that you never regret anything you do or don't do. It's the way to becoming a mature person. You must let go of the pain of the past to make space for a healthy and productive present and to build a better future. It will help you to get unstuck from the painful past.

IMITATING OTHERS

Imitating others without an inner compass is a surefire way to mediocrity, unhappiness and a miserable life. It is unhealthy for people to uncritically copy others or compare themselves to others in order to make sense of their life. The deeper meaning of this is: people consider themselves worthless. Individuals displace themselves from the center of their own life. This undervaluing of yourself and denying your right to become a serious actor in your own right is an offence against human dignity. By following this path, people live a life of conformity to social expectations. As they fail to think for themselves, their brain remains largely unused. There is a saying that an idle brain is the workshop of the devil. It leads people to useless thoughts and living a life of jealousy, frustration and bitterness.

Comparison to others drains people's creative energy and mental strength. When following this path, people direct blame for their own failures at their parents, siblings, colleagues, boss, community, state and politics. In the age of social media, people are digitally connected. However, this connection is superficial at the best. In this age of information bombardment, shouting has become the fashion. If you don't shout, people don't listen to you. The more you shout, the better attention you may get. That's why many people are prone to show off and brag about superficial things on social media. But deep inside they are unhappy, lonely, dislocated or depressed. They are the victims of poor family relations. Many people don't do their own thinking or act responsibly. As a result, others do their thinking. They become blind followers. That's why conspiracy theories are so popular nowadays. Some people believe that the world is conspiring against them to deprive them of their dues as a group. This group thinking is one of the major obstacles to personal growth. People fail to take an objective look at their true personal needs. They get trapped in group thinking. In this, focus remains misplaced. People react to circumstances without firmly locating themselves in the picture. For them, nothing seems to work. It's tragic indeed. It is the result of superficial living under the imagined protection of society – a child-like thought process. This is why the philosopher Ralph

Waldo Emerson urged people to be themselves and never imitate others.

To live an authentic life, you must discover yourself in the first place. It requires self-examination in order to attain self-knowledge and a self-directed life. You must prepare your life in the light of your values and priorities to defy the limiting opinions of others. Don't copy others blindly. If you do so, you will end up like the men who ran after a kite after hearing a rumor that the hunter bird had snatched away their ears. There is no doubt that you should trust others and live a sociable life. However, it is more important to check your ears before chasing after a bird together with others. You should never give others too much power over your personal life. Rather, you should develop faith in yourself. You must make your own choices based on your own needs and circumstances. By doing so, you can save yourself from being little more than a number only.

Looking primarily at yourself can be a good starting point for creating a positive mindset for success. To avoid mimicking others, you need to ignore the limiting demands of society. You have to keep faith in yourself. It will help you claim your individuality and to figure out a personalized solution to your own needs. Do yourself justice and stop blaming others for your misfortunes. Take ownership of your thoughts and actions. Develop an individual blueprint for life based on your own true strengths, needs and priorities. To take this step, you must take yourself seriously and claim your mental independence from the crowd to become true to yourself.

To fulfil your true potential, you must give up the passive

mode of thinking. You must take charge of your life. In the absence of your own goals and actions, your dreams are defined by the opinions of others. People live their lives to fit into dominant social expectations, undermining a personalized path of self-expression. Their focus in life remains misplaced. They fail to grasp the fact that to become successful, you need to take charge of your own life in the first place. Through pursuing a path of individual perfection, you can develop yourself and contribute to building community cohesion. It's a way forward to develop individuality, personal growth and fulfill your potential.

N.F.S. Grundtvig, the father of *Danish Folk High School* and Paulo Freire, the Brazilian educator and the pioneering figure of *critical pedagogy* for the oppressed, focused on the importance of giving voice to individuals. Though their writings were based on European and non-European contexts, their core philosophy is similar. They wanted to put individuals at the center of their life in order to make them active citizens. Grundtvig created a flexible lifelong learning method that aimed to make Danish people self-reliant, responsible and capable citizens. This life-changing educational philosophy has had a powerful impact not only in Denmark but also in other Nordic countries and beyond. Grundtvig is considered as the single most influential figure in formation of Danish nationalism.

TOO BROAD FOCUS

Very often, people's career, business or financial goals are too abstract, too general or too broad to achieve. It's great to be ambitious. There is nothing wrong with it. However, it is important to narrow down the focus to make things more actionable. To live a life without regrets, you must narrow down your focus and work towards specific goals. For this, you need to know where exactly you stand now in relation to your ideal career path. Then, you must find out your own skills and fill any gaps. There are so many things in life that occupy or distract our minds. You have to focus on the most important things based on your true priorities. To do yourself justice, you have to remove lower-value and less-productive things from your life. Only by getting your focus right, can you live a life of true passion.

INDIVIDUAL TALENTS UNDISCOVERED

All people are born unique. They are endowed with different inherent core gifts or capabilities. Thomas Carlyle had termed humans as the miracle of miracles. All people are naturally good in something. You may have noticed that some people can inherently learn and perform certain tasks effortlessly. If nurtured correctly, they can excel in their skills in a much shorter time than others. The role of teachers and parents is to identify the individual gifts of children and nurture these, so that they can fulfill their potential. However, it's an unfortunate truth that parents and teachers in many parts of the world fail to identify and nurture pupils' unique individual capabilities. Economic, cultural, political, class issues or quality of school systems can act as barriers. Instead of nurturing individual strengths, schools often focus on students' weaknesses. This focus on weaknesses make students average in performance as youths and adults. It's killing off their true potential. It's the cult of mediocrity in action.

In many contexts, schools fail to foster students' individual interests, strengths and needs. Instead of supporting talents and excellence, they undermine natural qualities and lower standards. It's such a waste of valuable human potential. The school system currently, as it exists in many parts of the world, don't serve the needs of all students. It serves the needs and expectations of a minority. It provides education that is too general and too abstract for the majority. It fails to provide useful knowledge and skills. The core philosophy of school systems is to create a set of students with similar taste, interest and outlook in order to serve national needs. Schools can do more to fill practical needs and aspirations of individual students. If they can do so, the world would be a far better place with less resentment and violence. Most of the problems of the world are directly related to this mismatch between an individual's true interests, education and career choice.

FEAR OF FAILURE

Generally, people see failure in a negative light. They see failure as a dead end. They try to avoid it at all costs. They are so cautious of failure that they hardly dare to live their lives. They don't realize the truth that failure is a useful experience for achieving success in life. Failure pushes people to test their limits in order to increase endurance. Used positively, it can help people in initiating life changes. It also helps you to develop the capacity for withstanding challenges. It makes you stronger. If you don't fail, you don't get useful insights and mental resolve to succeed. Failure is, in fact, a stepping stone towards success. If you look at the incredible success stories of the most successful and famous people from around the world, you will realize that they became winners by overcoming their fears. They successfully used their fear to fuel success. Despite facing extreme hurdles, they believed in themselves and their missions. Their economic, social or cultural conditions could not deter them from pursuing their dreams. Many used their rock-bottom failures and re-emerged as victorious.

To be successful, instead of seeing fear as an obstacle you must turn it into an opportunity for growth. It's a blessing in disguise. It is important that you try something new and aren't afraid to fail. Failures provide you with a valuable learning opportunity for success. They also strengthen your resolve to face uncertainty and danger to achieve your goals. This provides a valuable opportunity for pursuing personal growth. So, don't be afraid to fail. For success, you must give it a try. If you cannot achieve something with one try, then try five times. If you cannot do it with five attempts, try ten times. If you cannot do it with ten attempts, try a hundred times. But don't stop until you succeed. The world's greatest inventors and social reformers dared to fail in their ventures. By doing so, they contributed to making the world a far better place to live. Their dreams for invention and changing society had threatened the then dominant pattern of social thinking. As a result, many of them had been called queer, mad or crazy for their "abnormal" thinking and behaviour. However, the fire of their dreams encouraged them to defy social expectations, ridicule and even threats of violence. They each listened to their inner self.

Like any other people, they also experienced fear of failure. But they overcame it through the sheer power of their spirit, courage and committed action. They not only reached their goals but also changed the world. Thanks to their dreams, we live in a far better world now. They prepared themselves by using continual personal growth to make the impossible possible. If you want to achieve massive success, you must dare to fail. By trying and failing, you will get valuable experience in life. When you do that, you will have no regret in the future. Failing is a sign that you are alive. Only dead people never fail.

PROCRASTINATION

Who does not want to be successful? Everybody does. Then how come only a small percentage become successful and others live average or uninspiring lives? It is individual drive that separates successful from unsuccessful people. Continuous action is the key to achieving success. Even a slow tortoise can eventually win a running race against the fast but procrastinating hare. Slow and steady wins the race! Although most people wish to be successful, they fail to act on their goals due to over-analysis or lethargy. Deep down, people fear change. They look for stability. Fear of uncertainty and chaos stop them from adopting a new course in life. Due to procrastination, their work at hand becomes too enormous to handle. They prefer waiting for the "perfect" moment to arrive before they will take any action. But that perfect moment may never come. Or, if it comes at all, it comes too late. When people procrastinate, their knowledge and experience cannot help them. Procrastination lowers individual productivity and success.

People want to avoid failure and pain at all costs. However, from life stories of highly successful people, we learn that failure and pain have worked as opportunities in disguise. Painful experiences, humiliation and hopelessness forced them to take charge of their lives. For success, you must consider change as a natural part of life. You must take focused action with utmost discipline. The road to success is uneven, uncertain and at times extremely painful. To mentally prepare yourself for overcoming challenges, you must believe in your own dreams. This will help you to keep moving. You must decide and take the first step. You must adopt a flexible "trial and error" method to reach your goals. In order to consolidate success, you must celebrate your every small win. It will help you to break the cycle of failure. By doing so, you won't allow your circumstances to control you. Rather, you will control your circumstances. Your rising levels of self-confidence will enable you to move mountains. At this stage, the most important task is to take action – no more wishing and dreaming. In my childhood, I learned how to swim simply when my father threw me into the water! I learned to swim by actually doing it. So, no theorizing any more. You must act. Doing things will break the vicious cycle of procrastination. Take the first step to keep moving forward.

IGNORANCE ON THE PURPOSE OF LIFE

People often lose their perspective in the quest for material success. They collect pieces of glass at the expense of diamonds. Before taking any action, you must have a sense of your broader goal and where you want to go. Make sure that you really want to go there. For success, you need a clear roadmap prior to your journey. When you do not understand the nature of human life, you cannot find yourself in the context of community, society and broader humanity.

All humans are alike. We all have our own personal needs, dreams and aspirations. You cannot judge people only through your own self-serving lens. People are meant to be much larger than self-servers. To create a more meaningful and fulfilled life, you must become a contributing member of your family, community and broader humanity. Contributing to others opens up avenues for real success. It is said that humans are created in God's image. Human are created to love each other. Life is more about becoming a resourceful person, reaching individual perfection and serving others. Only through humility and clarity of purpose, can you attain honors and privileges. Understanding this truth will save you time and help you to live a purposeful life.

Most people naturally make self-preservation a priority. It is an in-built mechanism that helps people to survive in harsh conditions. At the same time, people are also altruists. So, stop being judgmental and harshly critical to others. Earning money is important for our basic survival, however, it is not the sole purpose of life. It's just a means for achieving other goals. Those who don't understand this may spend their entire life in pursuit of money. They may become millionaires or even billionaires. However, amidst material success, they may remain unhappy and unfulfilled. The world has its fair share of rich but unhappy people. Otherwise, no billionaire or celebrity would commit suicide. This brings up another issue for discussion. What makes people happy in life? To understand this, you must take a long hard look at life. You must understand the meaning, purpose, potential and limitations of life.

When you get a clear understanding of this, it will be easier for you to figure out your strengths and personalize your career and life goals. You will be able to achieve this in harmony with your value system. When you serve others and add value in others' lives, then you become truly successful. It will make you happy.

SELF-ASSESSMENT/ACTIONS

In your opinion, what is success?

1. ____

2. ____

3. ____

What are the three most important things in your life?

1. ____

2. ____

3. ____

What are three key obstacles that hold you back from pursuing a dream career?

1. ____

2. ____

3. ____

What three major habits are you ready to give up to build a career of your choice?

1. ____
2. ____
3. ____

What three major changes do you need to initiate for career success?

1. ____
2. ____
3. ____

What are the three things you have to do now to pursue the life of your dreams?

1. ____
2. ____
3. ____

CHAPTER 2

TIME-TESTED WISDOM ON SUCCESS

The human brain is the most sophisticated among all species of living beings in the world. Because of its extremely sophisticated processing power, it can also be termed as a miracle machine. By using its power of imagination and dreams, the human race has made a huge amount of progress. From the unprotected life of hunters and gatherers, humans adopted agriculture and rural settlements, built cities and moved towards industrialization. Over the passage of time, we have advanced in science and technology. We have come a long way from the age of the printing press to this Internet age. It is people's deepest desires and actions that have moved the wheels of progress. The power of their dreams, together with self-confidence, have made the world a better place. Ralph Waldo Emerson identified self-trust as the essence of heroism.

For an average person, a dream is something you have while

you are asleep. But for successful people, it cannot be that passive. For them, their dream is such a strong force that it can deprive them of their sleep. APJ Abul Kalam, the nuclear scientist and former President of India, who had humble beginnings, perceived dreams in this way: if you have a dream you believe in, you lose sleep until you achieve it.

This "burning desire" is one of the driving forces of success. Success is a mental state. People become successful because of their winning mindset. Success is not in short supply in the world. But millions of people fail because of the wrong focus or a negative mindset. As a result, a lifetime of hard work may prove futile. If this happens, it may become too hard to start life all over again in your old age. In a miserable condition, you may feel that your nearest and dearest and society have betrayed you. But in reality, you may have been a victim of your own making. But if you make such mistakes during youth or middle age, you may draw valuable lessons to take your career to new heights.

In this world, people are surrounded by problems. You have to keep in mind that every problem has a solution. By solving problems, people can make sense of their life. It requires common sense, as well as a creative mind and actions. However, common sense does not automatically come with educational degrees or maturity. Real wisdom is drawn from life experiences. You can create personalized goals using this wisdom. When you do so, you can turn your life around. To condition your mind for success, you need to get a perspective on nature, its potential and limitations. Considering this aspect of life and building a society of ideals, Plato, underlined the importance of the "philosopher king." Like a philosopher king, you can live a successful life based on wisdom, courage and reliability. This starts from knowing yourself, living a life of clear purpose and taking action. When you can do this, strength will spring up from within. You will not be overpowered by uninformed public opinion. You will see the bigger picture of life with a fresh pair of eyes. You will find your life connected to other human beings by a common thread. You will live a rich, compassionate, happy and fulfilled life. You will be at peace with yourself and the world. To do this, you have to know the following wisdom of life.

KNOW YOURSELF

Millions of people around the world fail to understand the nature and purpose of their lives. They live in the cocoon of ignorance. They fail to understand their own personal gifts and potential, and the ways in which they can use these to improve their lives. It's the result of people seeing life in a narrow context. They fail to spend time in self-reflection, self-criticism and self-initiative. It is a universal fact that, primarily, people act for self-interest and self-preservation. It is an important function of human life to protect yourself from outside dangers. In general, people don't live in jungles any more. We don't need to protect ourselves from wild animals or individually produce our own crops for food. In fact, we are living in a modern world with unprecedented wealth and living standards. In this age, life is much more easy and comfortable. Yet people are not grateful for their blessings. They live a life of gullibility and selfishness. It is the result of their unwillingness to think for themselves. This leads them to personal as well as collective miseries. They become the slaves to their own habits. Development of self-understanding can rescue people from this vicious cycle of lethargy.

By understanding human life in a broader context, you can recreate yourself as a credible individual. When you connect yourself to the community and beyond, you can develop empathy for others. By doing so, you can become a better person. You can survive temporary setbacks or disappointments with inner courage. You can realize that changes that come from within are real and sustainable changes. Knowing yourself will help you to take control of your fate. You will be able to pursue your goals by rising above the praise or blame of others. When you become a person of value, you attract positive interest, trust and success in life. However, you must pay a price for it. You must go much further than an average person is willing to go. When you can single-mindedly embrace a painful transformation process, it will produce marvelous results. This power to act will separate you from the rest. No one can take away this from you. To reach this state, all you need is to claim your individuality and demand higher standards from yourself.

Religious, philosophical and legal principles show us that we all are part of one humanity. We all are dependent on each other in a broader way. Individual success, in terms of money and fame, may not automatically translate into a happy or fulfilled life. Fulfillment is something bigger and deeper than material success. After achieving success, if you are still unhappy and miserable, you must rethink your approach. Fulfillment is something that gives life greater meaning. To achieve this, you must understand one of the key secrets of life: your happiness depends solely on yourself, not on others. The legendary biblical King Solomon prayed to God to grant him an understanding heart. Like him, you should cultivate this understanding for others in your character. It will save you from many avoidable mistakes and resultant troubles. Knowledge and wisdom are more important than money. You may lose money and material possessions, but you will never lose learning or wisdom. When you know who you really are – your strengths, your weaknesses – and have clarity of purpose, you are on your way to success in life. Prophet Muhammad said that the person who knew himself knew God. When you reach this mature mental state, you don't need to worry about how you appear in front of others. You will also stop unduly blaming yourself. This will awaken your subconscious mind, the sleeping giant within you. You will be able to achieve impossible things. It is not only the destination that will be rewarding – the journey itself will be enjoyable. As true friends are hard to find, first and foremost, be your own truest friend. When you do this, you will be able to create success, meaning and significance in your life.

UNDERSTAND OTHERS' NEEDS

Many people think that they are the sole center of the universe. In fact, generally, people are preoccupied with their own individual needs, expectations and survival instinct. There is nothing unusual about this. There is no difference between a king and a pauper in this respect. If you do the same bad things that others are doing, then what is special about you? To become truly successful, you need to remove judgement from your dictionary and to do your own best. You must understand other people's needs and become sensitive to their circumstances. Besides serving own interests, you must also become mindful of others' needs. When you add value in other people's lives, you become important to them. By doing so, you will develop leadership skills. You must treat people with empathy and try to solve their problems if you can. Serving others will help you to develop leadership qualities, a prerequisite for real success.

If you want to become truly successful, you must broaden your outlook in life. In your social setting, you may see that you have sacrificed a lot for others, yet instead of being grateful, they blame you for not doing enough. Keep in mind that it may have less to do with you: it is more to do with their own inability to fulfill their dreams. You can fulfill others' genuine needs, but not their willful expectations. In politics, we may see a leader being showered with rose petals today. However, within years, the same leader may get pelted with stones or eggs by the same group of people. If you intend to run for political office, you must know that rise and fall are a natural part of life. It's a matter of people's expectations. It is important that you do what is right and worry less about other people's reactions. If your conscience is clear and you carry out your responsibilities in the best possible way, no attack should hurt you. Understanding other people's emotions will make you a person with better insights. It's an important leadership quality that will help you to rise up the success ladder.

Some people are so much obsessed with themselves that they seldom have time to look at other people's concerns or points of view. If they are in the position of power, they cannot accept criticism. They prefer being flattered by their subordinates. This negative workplace culture may make them arrogant and insensitive to others. It may blur their vision so that they may not see things objectively. They may miss the point that irrespective of class and cultural differences, people belong to one human family. All parents of the world, it doesn't matter whether they are billionaires or beggars, think that their child is the most beautiful child of the world. So, when you deal with other people, you must understand their natural emotional needs in the first place. There is a Bengali saying that if you want to know whether a pot of rice is properly boiled or not, you don't need to check all rice in the pot. Rather, you can do it simply by checking just one grain. If you love your own kids, can you treat other people's children with cruelty or violence? When you understand yourself, you will understand the world. It will enable you to become compassionate to others. This human touch will make you a smarter and better person. Becoming a better person is a true measure of one's success.

SERVE OTHERS

In order to achieve true success and to give meaning to your life, you have to serve others. It cannot be earned by selfish possession of material things but by the spirit of our affinity with others. What you get in this world without serious effort is normally of low value or low quality. If you want to give someone something valuable, you have to nurture your own growth. A key difference between an average and a successful person is that the former wants to take as much as possible while giving the least in return. While self-seeking is necessary for individual survival, serving others opens up the avenues of real joy and greater fulfillment in life. What you give to others comes back to you multiplied in one way or another. Solving others' problems will increase your problem-solving skills and build your personal capacity. It will also enrich you spiritually. N.F.S. Grundtvig, M.K. Gandhi, Martin Luther King Jr, Oscar Romero, Mother Teresa and Paulo Freire dedicated their lives to the causes of education, non-violence, religion as service, social justice, humanitarianism and education for the poor. They left their signature on the world as a result of their remarkable contribution to humanity. They inspired millions of people around the world to carry the light of altruism, humanitarianism and global peace. They are iconic figures who dedicated their lives to the service of others.

If you want to remain an ordinary person, all you need to do is focus on getting educational diplomas and a regular job. It means selling one's monthly, weekly or daily time for a fixed salary. There is nothing wrong with being a salaried person. It is a life of self-centered living. However, if you want to create a fortune or personal significance, you must dedicate your time, energy and money to solving the problems of others. This can open up great business opportunities for you. By following this path, you can even become a billionaire! Serving others is a powerful tool for making yourself massively successful. To become massively successful, you need to fill an unmet need or serve an unserved or under-served people with something valuable. Bill Gates, Ted Turner and Steve Jobs did so by establishing Microsoft, CNN and Apple. By playing pioneering roles in their sectors, they became billionaires and influential people of the world.

If you want to be a millionaire or a billionaire, first you have to figure out why you want that much money. If your reason for attaining that money is only individual selfish reasons, rethink it. Maybe you are thinking about building the future for your sons or daughters. However, in the long run, leaving a large inheritance to your children can do them more of a disservice instead of helping them. Parents should rather focus on giving their children the right education, with useful personal and professional skills. As material wealth does not necessarily make a happy person, you should think about making your children people of values and principles. True success is about being in the service of others, particularly the less fortunate. Only selfless services can put you in someone else's heart and prayers. It's a question of becoming a compassionate and loving human being. This is the ultimate measure of one's success in life. By realizing this truth, Andrew Carnegie, one of the top American billionaires of the 20th century, donated a significant portion of his fortune to philanthropy in education, including building libraries and donating money for art and culture. He inspired several billionaires of our time to donate their money for charitable purposes.

There are many people around the world who work round the clock to change their societies for the better. They care for local, national and global community. However, the role of a vast majority of people remains limited to lip-service only. They don't give selfless service to others. Sometimes they become extremely critical to authorities. As they fail to walk their talk, their criticisms are nothing more than seasonal outbursts. They fail to build up a constructive dialogue. While criticism is important for bringing positive changes in society, it should not undermine the system itself. Rather, it should aim at improving things. Blaming for the sake of blame without taking individual responsibilities does not solve any problem. For solving a problem, critical engagement is important. Everybody should play his or her part. Playing one's own part is an important element of claiming one's stake in the community as well as a nation. It is far better than blaming and criticizing. If one has the will to serve, he can find ways. In my childhood, my primary school-educated mother used to encourage me to become a "real" human being. The role of a real human being, in her opinion, was to help suffering humanity by solving their problems. She said, "You should live a selfless life in helping others in a way that when you die, you will die in peace smiling and people will cry for you." To build such a life, words of criticism are not enough. You must do better than that. You must serve others and solve their problems with whatever skills you have got. This will create your personal relevance and significance in the world.

THE MINDSET OF ABUNDANCE

The world has plenty for serving human needs. It's mindset that enables or disables people to see and use these things. As family, schools and social institutions of many countries invariably promote the average as the ideal, this creates people of average mindset. In this mindset, people look for easy and short-cut solutions to everything. As the majority of people are after easy solutions to their problems, this creates a "scarcity mindset". This frame of mind is a barrier to innovation, entrepreneurship, cooperation and wealth generation in society. It is a fact that the world has an abundance of wealth. But people generally lack the vision, skills and ability to receive this.

The mindset of abundance encompasses an attitude of resourcefulness. It can produce miracles in life. With this mindset, a person doesn't see others as competitors in a rat race for scarce resources. Rather, he or she tries to improve their own skills and qualities to create value in the marketplace. You work on improving and bettering your past self. It's a journey into yourself. The focus in this case is not on money, fame or power. It's about the creation of your own excellence. Every success starts with a spark of imagination and dreaming. With the mindset of abundance, you see the world with eyes of positivity and abundance. You are ready to contribute to others. This attitude creates an imprint in the mind. Remember that leadership is a tool or an opportunity to help others. You don't necessarily need a formal position to become a leader. You can always serve others with or without a position.

Remember this.

GIVE MORE THAN YOU RECEIVE

In a world of shallow living, being self-seeking and self-serving is considered an important achievement. With this mindset, people want to benefit to the maximum by giving the least possible. In this selfish frame of mind, people focus on themselves only. There is little or no room for being mindful towards others. Human life, in its truest sense, is magical. It's a miracle. Love is the glue that holds families, societies and the world together. We create our value through connecting to others and contributing to them. When we act selfishly, we make ourselves small. We put small feet in big shoes. When we act selflessly, we become bigger. By positively contributing to others, we can find true happiness. From mere caterpillars, butterflies emerge as beautiful flying insects with wings, enjoying the nectar of flowers. Imagine the short lifespan of a butterfly: on average, one month for most species. However, they crucially contribute to the ecosystem as pollinators. They play an important role by contributing to the reproduction of plants and keeping environmental balance. Humans possess superior brain-power to think and change their condition. By working on yourself, you can increase your value in the marketplace and contribute to improve the lot of others. In gratitude for what you have received, you must give something back to others. When you are able to do this, you will feel good about yourself.

As there are less people who want to give more than they receive, you will find this path less crowded. As there will be little or no competition, you will be able to score in an empty field. By giving more in the service of less fortunate people, you will make yourself stand out among the crowd. This will increase your self-confidence, satisfaction and peace of mind. This is the high road to creating meaning in life. In this time of a rising tide of intolerance towards others, the principles of universalism can solve many problems of the world. The creation of empathy and sense of community can help building a rules-based world where everyone's interests are recognized and safeguarded. Instead of waiting for the world to change, you can adopt this principle individually to change the world. When individuals change, the world changes. It's a bottom-up process. Talking is not enough. This, of course, requires actions. Your actions should be valuable to others and contribute to giving them hope. By following this path, you can attract success in your life. This will give you much-needed inner peace. This legacy is not measured with money or wealth but with services provided to others. Let's say that from the nineteenth century onwards, hundreds of millionaires lived in this world. How many of them, would we know now? Those people who fail to use their wealth in service of others are forgotten when they die. Their tombstone may reflect that once upon a time, someone with their name lived in this world. That's it. Nothing more. How does that person matter to others? In contrast, those who use their wealth in the service of others continue to live in the hearts of people in the community, state and even globally. They are loved and respected. When you give more than you receive, you pave the way for wonderful returns even if you don't want them.

DON'T TAKE THINGS PERSONALLY

When you take a significantly different path from average people, invariably they will criticize you. They will question your judgment, ability or soundness of mind. Don't take other people's undue criticism of you seriously. Don't stop realizing your dreams because of the disapproval of random people. Consider the remarks of naysayers as mere opinions that have nothing to do with you. In fact, it may simply be a manifestation of their doubt in their own ability or a reflection of their jealousy towards you. It may have nothing to do with you. Don't listen to their negative opinions. Refuse to carry their negative baggage in your mind. The human mind is a powerful instrument. Don't stock garbage there. You must protect your mind from junk thoughts and keep it pure. It is possible to do so by practising personal discipline. For that, you must control your thoughts. Otherwise, your thoughts will control you. In that case, you will be most likely to have regrets in the future.

There are many types of people who are trying to make sense of their life. Some seek the easiest routes and short-cuts to advance their interests. They can use cunning, unethical and manipulative methods. In every society, unfortunately, you will find people like this at one stage or another in life. This may reflect their survival instincts. They may wear social masks or act in certain ways that they don't really believe in. It is said that before you own a seven-storey building, you should make the heart broad enough to own such a thing. Those who stoop low, you should not consider as bad or wicked people. Rather, you should feel sorry for them. There are many examples of Robin Hood-style noble thieves around the world who have carried out selfless and heroic acts for the good of society. They got placed in people's hearts and created legends. At the same time, people of "higher" social or moral standing can also act below their "standards". You have to think carefully whether you are immune from such faults yourself before being harshly critical of others. You have to develop an understanding of human needs, motivation and personality to understand what motivates others to act in a certain way. It will help you to develop people-reading skills to handle the real world without being judgmental. You must remember that no one is perfect. All people are works in progress. We are all in the same boat as far as our common humanity is concerned.

Life may not appear fair. You can be criticized even for doing good things. Should you react to such undue criticism? Of course not. In order to keep your peace of mind, you need to block negative people and their influence on your thoughts. You must filter out regrets, worries and resentments. Imbuing positive thoughts and actions will bring positive changes in your life. These will create better self-perception and improved self-confidence. To achieve this, you must filter out all negative thoughts and become kind to yourself and others. By handling different types of people, you will achieve emotional maturity. This will increase your understanding of the world and give you more problem-solving skills. It will enable you to see people as they are.

Joys and sorrows are a natural part of life. You should not be fearful about them. Rather, you should embrace them as opportunities for fueling personal growth. You should develop personal qualities or capabilities so that you may face problems more effectively. For this, you need align your life with values and principles. It will help you to rise above yourself and serve other people without expectations. It will make you credible to yourself. You will be fearless in facing any reality. When a person becomes trustworthy to himself, he lives in inner harmony. Then, he does not need to blame others to feel good about himself. Remember that you are not the center of the universe. There are millions of other people who live in this world. They also have their own aspirations, dreams and pain, just like you. We inherit our economic and cultural status as a result of our accidental birth in a certain family. There should be no pride or shame in a thing that we have not built ourselves. As a human being, you must understand this. When you understand this fact, you will not criticize others too harshly. You will be more graceful in your treatment of others. Increasing your level of tolerance to differences and different opinions will prepare you to take a larger role in society. It will help you to become a leader.

SCARCITY AND OBSTACLES PUSH YOU TO SUCCESS

If you read the life stories of great people in the world, you will find that the majority were not born with a golden spoon in their mouth at birth. With a humble start in life, they achieved remarkable feats through self-initiative and hard work under extremely challenging environments. Some failed over and over again and reached their lowest point before they had no option left but to succeed. They were hungry to change their situation. They used deplorable conditions – such as fear, pain or humiliation – to fuel extraordinary success. They used such conditions to fire up personal growth. Do you know that world-famous people such as Sylvester Stallone, Jennifer Lopez, George Soros, Oprah Winfrey, J.K. Rowling, Daniel Craig, Roman Abramovich, Lakshmi Mittal and Shahid Khan either grew up poor or became broke at least once? Several even faced homelessness for a period of their lives. Extremely difficult circumstances created a burning desire in them to become successful. They became obsessed with that and positively used their uncertainty, obstacles and scarcity to turn their lives around. These situations forced them to act decisively to get rid of deplorable conditions. It's the do-or-die situation that forces people to strive for greatness. When people take ownership of their life and work with sincerity, they pave the way for extraordinary success.

To become successful, you must perceive scarcity, obstacles and failures in a different way than the average person does. You should use these things to acquire new skills and experiences to outperform your past self. Hellen Keller, Louis Braille, Ludwig van Beethoven, Stephen Hawking and Michael Phelps all had one or other kind of disabilities. But they each defied their disability, pursued their own dreams and made history.

> Helen Keller, one of the best-known social activists, lost her sight and hearing at an early age. But disability could not stop her from pursuing her dreams. She is best known throughout the world as an advocate for people with disabilities.
>
> Despite his blindness caused by an early childhood accident, later in his life Louis Braille invented a system of reading and writing for blind or visually-impaired people. Named after him, this system is widely known as *braille*.
>
> Ludwig van Beethoven was one of the greatest composers and pianists of all time. After losing his hearing in early adulthood, the great composer single-mindedly focused on his passion for music.
>
> Stephen Hawking, one of the best-known scientists of all time, had a motor neurone disease that gradually paralyzed him over decades. In his early twenties, doctors gave him two years to live. But he became Professor of Mathematics at the University of Cambridge and lived to the age of 76.

The U.S. swimmer, Michael Phelps, is the most decorated Olympian of all time. He won twenty-three golds and a total twenty-eight Olympic medals altogether from 2004–2016. In his childhood, he was diagnosed with Attention Deficit Hyperactivity Disorder (ADHD), a learning disability in which you have trouble keeping focus. Humiliated in front of his school friends, he channeled his energy into swimming with focus and made Olympic history.

Being born in a rural family can also work as a disability in hierarchic societies. Born in a farming family of a Bangladeshi village, it was not easy for me to come to where I stand now. I spent my early childhood years in a village. Later, I lived in small towns and Dhaka, the capital city of Bangladesh. I got education from Dhaka University, the top university of that land. I had to wage a recurrent struggle to get there. When I was a ten-year-old schoolboy of fifth grade, one day I imagined my future. In my immature thinking, I counted that I would complete my secondary, higher secondary and BA examination (BA was the highest level of education then I could think of at that time) within seven years. Then I would get a job and establish a family. But things did not work out that smoothly. There was military or semi-military rule in Bangladesh during most of my student years. Survival in Dhaka University campus amid violent student politics was the greatest challenge. I was a survivor. But several of my fellow students got killed in the crossfire of gunfights. In addition to completing my Honors and Master's studies in the public administration department, I also worked as a campus reporter. I completed my education in Bangladesh eight years later than I had originally thought as a child. My studies did not stop there: they brought me to Finland. I completed my PhD from Helsinki University in 2004 – eighteen years later than my childhood calculation. Later, I worked as a senior researcher at Tampere University, taught at Helsinki University and worked in Finnish and international organizations. It is fair to say that my writing of this book is the direct result of professional uncertainties, as well as my burning desire to use my skills for greater social good.

SELF-EDUCATION IS THE TRUE EDUCATION

Some of the most original thinkers and world-class successful people did not go to a formal school or possess a diploma. They pursued steady and purposeful self-education in their chosen fields. While diploma-based formal education helps people with regular employment, lifelong self-education enables them to sharpen their practical knowledge and skills. In many societies, education has an academic bias. Graduates learn very few useful skills for everyday life beyond achieving status-symbol certificates. Very often, there is little qualitative difference in skills between an educated and an uneducated person. However, self-education is needs-based and practically-oriented. As this education is flexible and focused, it fills the real needs of a person. It can create fortunes for learners. The trailblazing industry leaders of any field are self-educated in addition to possessing formal degrees.

Born in poverty and obscurity, Benjamin Franklin, an eighteenth-century man rose to affluence and prominence not only in colonial America but also on the world stage as a statesman, diplomat, writer and inventor. The key to his success was self-education. From childhood, he was an avid reader.

Rabindranath Tagore was the great poet, novelist, song writer, philosopher, and the first winner of the Nobel Prize for Literature 1913 from Asia. He was born in a well-to-do cultural family with a strong link to the British colonial administration in India. Because of his drive for learning, he could use his family's strong financial standing to transform himself into a well-read man. He was a self-educated man without a formal diploma. He had read a lot and widely travelled within British India, as well as in Europe, America and the world, since his childhood. Tagore's towering intellectual influence reigns supreme even today, not only in India, Bangladesh or Asia, but around the whole world. He was the composer of the national anthem of both India and Bangladesh.

TIME: THE MOST VALUABLE RESOURCE IN LIFE

Time is the most precious commodity in life. In essence, it is life itself. The way you spend your time ultimately dictates your success or failure. You cannot get back bygone time even by surrendering all your accumulated wealth. In old age, people don't regret material possessions. Rather, they regret giving less time to what truly mattered most to them. They regret not pursuing the profession of their choice and not giving enough time for family and social good. They wish they could return to the past to correct their mistakes and lead a life of true priorities based on later wisdom. But it's impossible to return to the past. You also cannot hold back time. However, you can use the present based on your true priorities. As you cannot change the past, it makes no sense to regret past failures. One good way of using the past is as a lesson for the future. Today is the perfect day for you to take control of your time and create a more effective version of yourself.

Rich and poor, all people of the world have the same allocation of time – 24 hours a day, seven days a week, around 30 days a month and 365 days a year. You should use your time prudently based on your true personal priorities. When you look at average people, you realize that most of them can't fathom the value of time. They spend hours every day in useless socializing with others. Those activities, though they may have some social meaning, are devoid of purpose. It's a complete waste of valuable time, energy and money. For every action, you must have a good purpose. My late paternal grandfather Asmat Ali Doftori, a proud man in positive sense, had given me as well as my cousins a valuable piece of advice: "Don't go to a feast in expectation of eating tasty foods without first eating at home. You are not going there to fill your belly but to bring honor to the family." If you can use your time for personal development, this will yield better results in your career and life. For this, you must take control of your time and use it for what really matters in life. It will add value and change your life for the better. The correct use of time will fill the gap between your dream and your current state.

In this chapter you have been given an understanding of why people fail to live up to their true potential, as well as time-tested wisdom on success. This will help you to put your life in a broader perspective. It will help to remove misconceptions about life, its priorities and what it really means to become a successful person. This will help you to draw valuable lessons and build up a life of purpose and meaning. Based on this, you will be able to set your life goals. As success is not a zero-sum game, you can be as successful as you want. There is no limit to it. In fact, many people lack the capacity to attract success. To create a successful life, you must follow your passion. Without passion, life becomes mechanical and superficial. That's why whatever you do as a profession, you must do it with passion. Don't think that you have ample time to spare for useless things. In fact, your time is limited. Make the best use of it. It is said that when people have teeth, they don't understand their value. But when they lose them, they understand their true value. Don't be too late to understand this simple truth. Spend your time for things that truly matter in life. This will take you to the highway of success.

SELF-ASSESSMENT/ACTIONS

List the names of three heroes/heroines in your life.

1. ____

2. ____

3. ____

In your opinion, what are the three key values required for a successful life?

1. ____

2. ____

3. ____

What are the three most important things for pursuing a successful career?

1. ____

2. ____

3. ____

What are the three personality traits/habits that hold you back from a successful career?

1. ____

2. ____

3. ____

What are the three key personality traits you want to cultivate to build up a successful career?

1. ____

2. ____

3. ____

CHAPTER 3

THINK POSITIVE

THE POWER OF POSITIVE THINKING

Every person is born with unlimited potential. But the vast majority of the people in this world do not realize that each of them possesses unique and valuable gifts. Even if some know this, they fail to use this knowledge as a result of different limitations. By finding and using this, they can advance their career to new heights. It's like people breathing oxygen and yet unaware of its valuable function in supporting life. Human potential starts with the use of thoughts or imagination. People's imagination is like a pair of wings that are tested and strengthened the more they are used. People who can use their imagination and stick to their dreams become successful. They are makers of their own fate. James Allen considered the character of a man as the complete sum of his thoughts. Those who lack imagination live an average life. People without purpose end up living a shallow and unhappy life. Success starts with a positive mindset.

Unfortunately, the majority of people in the world suffer from social conformity. This creates doubt about their abilities. It leads to fear, self-contempt and poor self-confidence. This makes their lives aimless, unhappy and miserable. Their happiness depends on others. They blindly copy others and fail to take responsibility for their own actions and inactions. They blame others for their misfortunes. They hardly realize that they have power over their own minds. Simply by changing their way of thinking, they can pursue a new life of success. Changing your life to a positive direction is a matter of personal choice. Being true to oneself is of paramount importance. Ralph Waldo Emerson perceived the integrity of the human mind as sacred. You must protect it by every means possible.

The first step to changing yourself is to build up the right mental attitude. Mental attitude builds up people's self-perception, one of the most important determinant factors in success or failure. Negative mental attitude conditions you for failure and positive mental attitude conditions you for success. You should have gratitude for the blessings of your life. When you appreciate your blessings, you attract positive energy into your life. This will also be reflected in other aspects of your personality and behavior. This will help you to create positive inner transformation, a precondition for real success. The people you befriend and interact with in everyday life have a strong psychological influence on you. As friends have significant influence on your thinking, it is important that you choose your friends carefully. In order to save yourself from negative influences, you should have a filtering system in your mind. This system should keep negative people out of your life. There is a Bengali saying that if you put a single drop of cow urine in a bowl full of milk, the milk will get spoiled. When you keep a distance from negative people and environments, it will make space in your mind for positive influences. When you befriend positive people, their thoughts, routines and habits will have a positive influence in your life.

As positive thoughts produce positive results and negative thoughts produce negative results, it is important that you control your thinking. Whatever type of thoughts you repeatedly have, these will become ingrained in your mind. Your positive thoughts will attract positivity and your negative thoughts will attract negativity. For success, you must accept yourself, be positive in outlook and be authentic to yourself. You must remove negativity and fear from your life. To do this, you have to change your personal philosophy and embark on a new path. In this new path of positive thinking, you can create a life of possibility. You can put positive thinking to words, words to action, actions to habits, habits to character and character to destiny. Through this process, you can attain self-knowledge, self-confidence, resourcefulness and attract success in life. By pursuing this path, you can discard your worries about what others think about you.

Positive thinking is a powerful force that can fuel success in your life. To walk on this terrain, you have to take full responsibility for your thoughts and actions. It will give your life authenticity, substance and meaning. Many family, social and political problems do not stem from lack of money but from lack of imagination and more precisely, lack of positive thinking. You may have noticed that in your society, there are people who despite possessing good money and social status, live unhappy and miserable lives. You may also have noticed that there are some unique people who despite economic hardships and low social status become successful and inspire others. The first group lack resourcefulness and the latter group possess it. Resourcefulness is the thing that separates the two groups. Positive thinking is the starting point of inner resourcefulness and personal power. When you build up a habit of positive thinking, it will become a natural part of your personality. It's an ongoing process that requires time. It's never too late to start that process. We cannot control powerful forces that shape our reality. However, we can change our personal response to those realities. By positive thinking, we can transform challenges into opportunities.

Your mind is as holy as a church, synagogue, mosque or a temple is to the believer. You must protect the sanctity of it at all costs. It is a process that takes time and discipline. You cannot reach such a mental state overnight. It's not a fight against an external enemy in which you can declare yourself a winner. It's a fight against your inner limitations. This requires a self-directed purposeful change from within. You must take ownership of your mind and discipline it. You must refine yourself as a person and set new standards. You should manifest a positive attitude and kindness towards others. The only person you can be harsh with is yourself. This will open up a life of true living. To achieve this, you should give time to yourself. You can also embrace solitude.

Most people fail to put themselves at the center of their life. They often run here and there for socializing without a clear focus. They aim to feel good or safe with the social approval or validation of others. This gives them justification for their shallow existence. In the truest sense, it neither serves them nor their local or national community. Though they may live surrounded by many people, yet, deep inside they may feel empty and insecure. There are exceptional people who don't seek solutions to their problems by embracing the crowd. In fact, they avoid the crowd and to seek solitude in order to concentrate on their own thoughts and ideas. They save their time for ideals, values and principles to create their own personalized dreams. Artists, poets, writers and most creative people belong to this category. For success, you need to embrace this valuable process of solitude.

THE FINNISH MIRACLES

Finland is a Northern European nation situated between Sweden and Russia. It has a population of 5.5 million. It's a member of the Nordic Council. Other members of the Council are Denmark, Iceland, Norway and Sweden. Finland joined the European Union (EU) in 1995. The country got its independence from the Soviet Union in 1917. By leaving behind its painful history of foreign domination, wars and geopolitical uncertainties, it has emerged as a modern industrialized nation. It is one of the leading nations on earth in terms of high living standards, education, health, welfare and gender equality, peace and happiness. It is one of the top countries of the world according to many international surveys such as:

- World Happiness Report (Finland is ranked as the happiest country of the world in 2019)

- Stable country in Fragile States Index of the Fund for Peace
- Transparency Index of Transparency International
- World Press Freedom Index of Reporters Without Borders
- Prosperity Index ranking of The Legatum Prosperity Index
- Better Life Index of OECD
- Programme for International Student Assessment (PISA) ranking of OECD

From a farming nation, Finland has evolved into a remarkably-successful industrial nation in seven decades or so. The First Lady of the country goes to the same public maternity hospital as any other citizen or resident for giving birth to the presidential baby. There, she gets the same equal treatment and world-class services as everyone else. For people in many parts of the world, it may seem like a fairy tale. But it is true. Ministers of Finland move publicly without security personnel around. There is no exhibitionism of power or special travel arrangements for powerful people by blocking street traffic. All the above-mentioned feats have been possible due to Finnish people's creative mindset, hard work, resilience, pragmatism and commitment to democracy. It's a land of social justice where every citizen has the chance to pursue his or her own dreams without hindrance. In 2017, Finland celebrated one hundred years of independence. To celebrate this very special day in national life, a new Central Library in Helsinki, named Oodi, was opened in December 2018. It stands near the national

Parliament House. It is remarkable not only for its architecture and huge collection of books, but also for its accommodation of space for public events and meetings. It's a successful feat for a nation of book lovers.

Finland is internationally known for its epic Kalevala and Nokia, the erstwhile largest mobile phone maker of the world. Recently, it has become well known for its gaming industry. The best known among them is Rovio's Angry Bird series of games. Major internationally-known Finnish companies include Kone, Metso, Valmet and Wärtsilä among others. Finland is a peace-loving and peace-promoting nation. It has a Peace Station in Helsinki's Pasila district which houses peace organizations such as the Peace Union of Finland. Helsinki, Finland's capital is well known for hosting negotiations of Cold War rivals of NATO and Warsaw Pact countries led by the two superpowers, the U.S. and the Soviet Union. In 2018, it also hosted the summit between the U.S. President, Donald Trump, and Russian President, Vladimir Putin. Finland's former President, Martti Ahtisaari, is well known throughout the world as a high-profile peacemaker. He played a prominent role in conflict resolution in Namibia, Kosovo, Indonesia and Iraq. As a recognition of his peacemaking role in the world, in 2008, he was awarded the Nobel Peace Prize. Pekka Haavisto, the Minister for Foreign Affairs of Finland, is also an internationally-known peace negotiator.

Since the independence of Finland, Finnish people have achieved enviable success in many sectors of national development. One can attribute their success to their indomitable spirit. In Finnish, it is called *Sisu*. When a nation can turn its positive vision into determined actions, it can achieve any feat such as those of Finland. Education is one of the most powerful tools that have transformed this nation into what it is now. Education is free in Finland. The Finnish comprehensive school system is run by highly-qualified and highly-trained teachers with state-of-the-art pedagogical methods. Craft education was first thought of and introduced as a compulsory subject in Finland in the 1860s by Finnish educator Uno Cygnaeus who is considered as the father of the Finnish public school system. Otto Salomon, a Swede, further developed and popularized the model of Cygnaeus, also known as *Sloyd* education, to the world. Craft education has contributed to Finnish people's love for technical and social innovation, as well as entrepreneurship development. The introduction of Folk High Schools, Study Circles and other adult education also played key role in creating a learning society. Those created the social basis for democracy at grassroots level. As public libraries of Finland are an integral part of the community, it contributes to creating well-informed citizenry. Though Finland is a small country, the rest of the world can learn a lot from it. The Finnish success story is all about the positive outlook, vision, determination and discipline of a people. It's about creating a true national community based on mutual support and trust. The same success principles can be applied at national, as well as individual personal levels too. By following this path, anybody can master personal development and achieve massive success in career and life.

LESSONS FROM MAHATMA GANDHI

Mahatma Gandhi's life practices reflected his message. He was a man of his word who walked his talk. He brought about huge change in the world through his philosophy of non-violence. His concept of non-violence is not about passivity but about deploying a powerful moral force for bringing personal and social change. To pursue this path, Gandhi practiced self-denial, non-cooperation, and civil disobedience – accepting arrests and imprisonments. His thinking, saying and doing were all in harmony. Through using the positive thoughts, a tradition-bound and shy Indian, Gandhi, gathered a wealth of knowledge and experimented with truth. He had dedicated his life to the service of a voiceless people and transformed himself into a *"Great Soul"*. He shook the world in a gentle way. South Africa played a formative role in Gandhi's experiments with non-violence as a method of fighting the unjust.

He used the painful experience to initiate non-violent protest against apartheid itself involving the Indian community in South Africa. By doing so, he shook the powerful British Empire in a positive way. From his autobiography, we learn that he defied threats of arrest, imprisonment and related physical and psychological pain. He returned to India after living two decades abroad. There, he led a non-violent movement against British colonial rule. He united Indians by healing ethnic, linguistic, religious and other divisions and dedicated his life to the cause of equality, justice and dignity for all. He became a prophet of non-violent social change. Towering moral figures such as Khan Abdul Gaffar Khan, Martin Luther King Jr., Rosa Parks, Nelson Mandela, Vaclav Havel and peace movements around the world got their inspiration from Gandhi's non-violent methods of social change. Gandhi raised a broader struggle against the social injustice of colonialism to force the British to leave the subcontinent peacefully.

Inspired by Gandhian ideals, Rosa Parks and Nelson Mandela courageously fought injustices in their homelands. the USA and South Africa. Parks, a black woman defied the unjust racial segregation law in Montgomery, Alabama, by refusing to give up her bus seat to a white passenger. It was in 1955. For her civil courage and defiance to the unjust racial segregation law, she faced arrest and trials. But her role paved the way for the birth of the civil rights movement led by Martin Luther King Jr., a Montgomery bus boycott for a year, and ultimately, the repeal of the racial segregation law in the US.

Mandela dismantled apartheid from South Africa without resorting to violence. He dedicated his life to ending racial discrimination and injustice in his country. From his life, we learn that he lived twenty-seven years in jail – accepting the fact that he might spend the rest of his life in the notorious prison of Robben Island. He was awarded the Nobel Peace Prize in 1993, together with Frederik Willem de Klerk, for his contribution to the peaceful termination of apartheid and for laying the foundation for a democratic South Africa.

Following Mahatma Gandhi's philosophy, you too can build

up positive changes in your life no matter how bad a shape you are in. When you nurture the right attitude, you can transform your reality from hopelessness to courage. When you develop a positive mindset, you can look at every situation with the eyes of possibility. It may not only change you, but also become a catalyst to change the world around you. In your eyes, the glass will appear half full, not half empty. You will develop inner resolve to overcome challenges without being overwhelmed by problems. With a positive mindset and actions, you will add value to your work. You will be able to make something out of nothing. You will even be able to create solutions in extremely hopeless situations.

THE MINDSET OF SUCCESS

Positive mental attitude is the first step for initiating personal development – it doesn't matter what condition you are in. If you can clearly identify a problem and take steps to address it, you can change it. Through positive mental attitude, you can create self-confidence that will lead you to success. You must take steps to empty your mind of negative thoughts and fill it with positive thoughts. Regular practice of positive thinking will make this a natural part of your personality. When you visualize yourself in a desired condition and act upon it, you will be able to realize your dreams. This can re-program your mind for success. To do this, you have to be grateful for the blessings of your life. If you are healthy, eat and sleep well, have family who care for you, you are better off than many people in the world. You are luckier than many kings, queens, presidents and prime ministers. Powerful people invariably lose these taken-for-granted privileges while in office and even afterwards due to security and other protocols. Imagine yourself in a situation where you cannot eat food before a food taster has tasted it, you cannot go and meet people without security clearance and your talks are scripted! There are some people who can defy government protocols to reflect their own personal choices.

Jose Mujica, the austere and charitable former president of Uruguay, considered as the world's poorest president, is a notable exception to this. Despite holding the highest office in his country, he lived a frugal life. Political leaders and celebrities are also individuals with human needs just like you and me.

Bangladesh's President, His Excellency Abdul Hamid, reached the top constitutional post of the republic after a humble beginning in a village. He served as a people's representative for decades. He is a very frank and jolly person who often speaks honest truths that surprise a section of people.

All people have different blessings in life. Good health and the love of family and friends are valuable gifts of life. Unfortunately, many people don't understand this truth. They think they have a right to these relationships. As a result, they fail to appreciate these gifts in life. If and when those things are lost, people understand their true value and meaning. To live a balanced and happy life, you need to be grateful for those gifts and compassionate to those less fortunate than you are. Many people see only with their eyes and lack the vision to see their lives in a broader context. To get that vision, you have to rise above yourself. Everybody has some negative experiences in life. Bad things can happen to anyone at any stage. But it is of utmost importance how you respond to this. Positive mindset is very important in this regard. Bhagavad Gita, the Hindu holy book tells believers to look at people with superior ideals and qualities. It asks people to look at role models who can return love for hatred and can forgive. Vision is a precondition for creating a reality. You can start this at any time. Believing in yourself is the starting point of this. When you can embark on this transformational journey, you will cease to live a superficial life. You will live a life of substance.

FROM NEGATIVE TO POSITIVE MINDSET

Family, as well as educational and social institutions, all play a major role in shaping people's mindset. Negative mental attitude attracts negative thoughts and actions. These lead to a life mistrust, frustration, bitterness and misery. But it's possible to change from a negative to a positive direction. If you are charting a new path of success, it is important that you avoid unhappy and complaining people. Bad things can happen to anyone. These give people pain. But bad things of the past should not define you. As a human being, you are meant to be much bigger than your problems. People have the gift of "willpower" to turn things around and create a different reality. Used correctly, this can lead people to success. According to the Quran, the Muslim holy book, humans are created in the best form and endowed with the spirit of God. They are miniature Gods on earth with will-power, the power to choose. That's why after creating Adam, the first man on Earth, God ordered angels, the fiery spirits, to bow down before him. All complied except *Iblis*, the most favored angel of God. He defied this divine order out of jealousy for the earthly Adam.

As humans have free will, the superior gift they are in control of is shaping their own destiny. The true source of success is a desire or a dream. People have the power to give shape to their dreams. In order to access this power, you must possess or develop a positive mindset. This can be achieved through positive attitude, self-discipline and persistence. To live a positive life, you need to unlearn negative thoughts and give space for positive thoughts and habits. First and foremost, it's a matter of conscious decision. Success is, in fact, a habit or mindset not a destination. It's an internal process. To become successful, you must work on yourself. The following steps will help you to bring about positive changes in life.

BE GRATEFUL

To get rid of negative thoughts and adopt a positive mental attitude, you need to attain a certain degree of self-understanding in the first place. This will help you in leading a life of higher purpose and meaning. You have to be grateful about all gifts in your life. Life is beautiful – it's a miracle in its truest sense. The older you grow, the more you realize the true nature of life. Sometimes it may appear to you that the world is full of self-seeking, greedy and manipulative people. However, when you are in friendship or fall in love, you don't judge these people. You take a softer approach in dealing with loved ones. In reality, the world may appear good or bad based on our own moods and interpretations of particular situations. If you are in good health, you have good reason to be happy. What's the value of lots of money, social prestige or celebrity status if you don't have good health to enjoy them?

Generally, people are generous and good at heart. They reciprocate the kind gestures of others. It is universal that people adore a baby, a beautiful flower and a butterfly. Despite all difficulties of life, people take care of other human beings that they love. If you are in good health, have a house to live in and family to support you, you are living a privileged life. Millions of people around the world are not blessed with these privileges. There are some countries and regions of the world where people suffer from hunger, famine, malnutrition, lack of education, outbreak of preventable diseases, lawlessness or war. Imagine: there are millions of children around the world who still suffer from malnutrition, are homeless or live in urban slums. Children are also victims of war. Some are forced to become child soldiers or separated from their families in foreign lands. Thousands of children still die from preventable diseases. If you are not suffering from such emergencies, you should be grateful for the blessings of your life.

The modern news media is flooded with negative news coverage. Their coverage of news creates an impression that the world is full of crimes and crooks and hopelessness. They mostly fail to portray people in positive light. Because of great human progress in science and technology, we live in a better world now compared to any other time in human history. Despite certain tragic situations in some corners of the world, we are much better off than ever before in terms of access to food, education and healthcare. Because of worldwide campaigns of civil society organizations, the world is moving in a better, positive direction. Think about the effects of the International Campaign to Ban Landmines, the International Campaign to Abolish Nuclear Weapons (ICAN), the Global March against Child Labour, the Jubilee Debt Campaign, the Global Campaign for Climate Action (GCCA), the Millennium Development Goals (MDGs), the Sustainable Development Goals (SDGs) and many other campaigns. These campaigns create a ray of hope for the hopeless. They prove that human beings are altruistic by nature.

Individually, you should give up negative thoughts and find out what's working in your life. You should be grateful for your blessings. Instead of blaming wicked people for the wrongs of the world, try to see how some remarkable people, despite facing obstacles, are contributing towards changing the world for the better. Their spirit will show you that there are reasons to be optimistic. When you look at this side of humans, you cannot be too cynical or lose faith in people any more. You should change your outlook on suffering and struggles. This can help you in building up your inner strength and fuel greater success in life. You too should contribute to local, national and global change. Your small contribution may have bigger meaning to some people. Life is beautiful. It must be celebrated. Express your gratitude to God or whatever unseen force you believe in. Extend a helping hand to people less privileged than you. People who come back to life from near-death experiences invariably say that they will be kinder and fairer in dealing with others in future. So, be kind to people in everyday life before it's too late. A small act of kindness or help may mean something big for others. When you give, it comes back to you in one way or another, even though you may not seek any reward. So, be generous with others.

You don't need to be extremely rich to be kind. Your willingness is enough. If you don't have anything else to give, greet others with a broad smile. It will help the other person to begin the day positively. Think about Mother Teresa, a Macedonia-born Albanian-Indian Roman Catholic nun and missionary, who dedicated her life for selflessly helping the poorest of the poor – such as those dying with HIV/AIDS, leprosy and tuberculosis. Imagine how little an average person does to help fellow human beings in dire need. Helping others can give you mental satisfaction and peace. To do so, all you need is a caring heart.

PREFER KNOWLEDGE AND SELFLESSNESS

Knowledge is the stepping-stone towards success. With knowledge, you can lead a life of vision and purpose. Despite possessing fortunes, some people still fail to become happy in life due to a lack of knowledge. Knowledge cannot be earned easily. Getting true understanding of oneself may be too scary for feeble minds. It kills illusion and puts us in front of reality as it is. This, together with skills will kill your doubt and fear. It will transform your life into a successful one. It's a self-driven process. As it is highly valuable, you cannot expect to earn it being at ease. You must go through a painful process to earn it. It's less about gaining materials and more about becoming a person of knowledge, skills and competence. Excessive materialism cannot bring true fulfillment in life; it is important to cultivate the personal virtues of mind and character.

You cannot change the past and outer realities of the world. But you can definitely change yourself. It is possible to improve yourself without comparing yourself with others. To change yourself, you need to change your habits in the first place. With new habits, your personality changes. You have to renounce negative thoughts and habits in order to instill a positive habit. Positive habits will help you to fulfill your goals in life. Inner changes will lead you to outer changes. Only the changes from within are sustainable. The process of change is often painful and time-consuming, but the results are highly rewarding. Outer change without inner compliance is like wearing a new dress only. It has no substance. Inner change is like lighting a candle to help you find your own way at night-time instead of cursing the darkness. You can share the light with as many people as possible without losing your own.

When you earn knowledge, you see the world with the eyes of an adventurer. By connecting dots, you can create something new and powerful that others may not imagine. Knowledge itself is not powerful. Had it been so, our world would be ruled only by university professors or experts who produce and control knowledge. But this is not the case. Therefore, relatively less-educated and apparently less-qualified, less-experienced and more courageous people often assume leadership in various fields. Every day the world is made better by millions of selfless people of different crafts and professions who reach out and serve others. They make a positive impact on other people's lives. Think about health professionals, social workers and schoolteachers around the world who silently serve others and contribute to greater change in society.

A Bangladeshi friend of mine, Bodiuzzaman Mukul, like me, pursued his higher studies in Finland. Later, he moved to Canada as an immigrant and became a citizen of that country. A truly selfless person and a good reader, he found the profession he truly loves. He is a mental health professional working in Toronto. In addition to his professional duties, he voluntarily reaches out to immigrants, offering them valuable advice as part of his passion. He was shortlisted for the RBC's Canadian Immigrant Award. He uses his passion, knowledge and skills to improve the lives of others. As no one is perfect, you should not fear making mistakes. Knowledge and skills are a "trial and error" process. This process will lead you to personal growth and success.

KNOW YOUR WHY

In life, everyone has a different target, goal and ambition that he intends to achieve. Some reach these but the majority fail to do so. What's the difference between a successful and an average person? It's the burning desire that separates successful from less successful people. If someone pursues a goal for the sake of money or to meet social expectations without an inner calling, they may retreat from their goal when challenges arise. Outer-oriented motivation fails to provide a sense of purpose and direction in life. To live an authentic life, you need to create a tailored profession of your choice that fits your personal interests, strengths and circumstances. It's a matter of clarity about the purpose of your life. However, millions of people live a superficial life of impulses and desires without ever knowing what their true calling is. Successful people take control of their mind. They take the necessary action to turn their personal dreams into reality. They consider mistakes as a learning opportunity for future improvement. It's an individual growth process that can truly help you in developing yourself.

Without a higher purpose in life, money alone cannot give you happiness and fulfillment. However, if you can relate your goals to something bigger or greater than your individual self, you can face challenges more effectively. This higher purpose depends on your value system. It's about what people truly value. It may be one's family, community, humanity, God or something similar. By connecting yourself to a higher cause, you can overcome hurdles. This can have a lasting influence on your personal motivation and grit. It is an unfortunate fact that millions of people die without ever discovering their true selves and their true potential. It's tragic.

When you don't know this about yourself, how can you pursue a suitable career based on your true passion? As an expert on international education, I conducted research in several states of South Asia and sub-Saharan Africa. There, I saw highly-talented children and youths who could not fulfill their dreams due to poverty and social customs. They were like buds that dried before blooming into flowers. But some turned around their lives by enrolling in non-formal and technical education. I found Bangladesh Rural Advancement Committee (BRAC)'s Non-Formal Primary Education (NFPE) and Underprivileged Children's Educational Program (UCEP), Bangladesh's technical and vocational education, the most effective among many non-governmental organizations (NGOs) in South Asia and sub-

Saharan Africa. The major reasons behind the success of the two NGOs were their needs-based and skill-oriented educational curricula. They know what they are doing and why they are doing it.

In my ancestral village, there was a man in his forties in my neighborhood during my study years at Dhaka University. Whenever I visited my home, travelling from Dhaka, I listened to BBC Bangla Radio in the mornings and evenings. A lay fisherman came and sat beside me on a chair and listened with keen interest to the BBC news and news analysis on Bangladesh and world politics. He truly cared about the people of the world and world peace. He often asked me thought-provoking questions. But he had never attended a school and could not read and write. If his family had been better off and if he could have received an education, he could have been a great ambassador of world peace. People of my ancestral village, and Bangladeshi people in general, are economically far better off now compared to the first half of the 1990s. But unfortunately, the education system of Bangladesh still fails to discover and nurture talents, like many other countries. That's why so many people fail to fulfill their true potential.

SURROUND YOURSELF WITH THE RIGHT PEOPLE

Our friends and companions reveal so much about us. Usually people mix with other people with similar thoughts and interests. People are social animals. We easily get influenced by our friends and surrounding environment. Outside family members and teachers, we are highly influenced by our friends on decision-making for career and other important life decisions. As you cannot choose your family, it is important that you choose your friends carefully. Friends play an important role in influencing your values, outlook and behavior. Negative friends can infect your life with negative values, attitudes and habits. Conversely, positive friends can inspire you with positive values, attitudes and habits. To become successful in your career, you must shun the influence of negative people and fill your life with positive ones. There is a Bengali proverb that the right companion can lead you to a heavenly existence and the wrong one can ruin you.

During my years at *Titumir College* in Dhaka, Bangladesh, I stayed at the college hostel. There, I had the opportunity to build a collaborative relationship with some of the most ambitious and talented students of the college.

We seven to eight students lived in a four-seat room. For the sake of improving our English language skills, we subscribed to an English daily instead of a Bengali daily. For this, I used an English-Bengali dictionary and memorized English synonyms and antonyms. We prepared for the admission test at higher educational institutions. We shared our knowledge and experience with our friends on a regular basis. With one, I always talked in English. The result of this positive environment was clear to me. I got admission to the department of public administration at the University of Dhaka, for one of the most prestigious subjects of the university. All my inner circle of friends got admission in the top general, engineering and medical universities or colleges of Bangladesh. Later, they joined elite cadres of the Bangladesh civil service – such as diplomatic, police and public administration cadres. Others became doctors and engineers. Several got selected as cadet officers of the Bangladesh armed forces. Saleh Uddin, my best friend in the college and one of the key initiators of the collaborative relationship, is now a senior officer in the Bangladesh Navy.

RISE ABOVE YOURSELF

Historically, all great achievers of the world rose above their limitations to achieve greater success in life. It's about taking yourself to a new height by defying the challenges. With burning desire, together with clarity of purpose, action and discipline, you can reach your goals. Behind every success, people usually have a compelling reason that pulls them forward. The level of motivation depends on your type of personality. When meaningful personal emotions are deployed in achieving a goal, the reason for success becomes compelling. In this situation, your subconscious and conscious mind work in harmony to achieve your goal. In a passionate state, you push yourself forward to seize the moment.

Average people live self-centered lives and spend most of their time fighting for everyday survival. They opt for the easiest and most crowded route. This makes their life complicated. They get trapped into a vicious cycle of mediocrity. They do average things and compete with others for limited opportunities. Though some of them may attempt to do selfless acts occasionally, their lives revolve around complaining and quarrelling. A self-centered life is a surefire way to mediocrity. If you want to be truly successful, you must expand your horizon. You must serve others and contribute to solve their problems. The majority of people are overburdened with own problems and don't have time to serve others. To move towards success, you have to walk the less-crowded path. When you can walk this path, it will build up your individuality. You will be able to act responsibly towards others. It's very important for success. When you serve others, it enables you to gain personal significance in addition to a material fortune. When you can connect your past thinking with pain and your future with something desirable, it will push your life in the right direction. It's an ongoing process. When you are able to connect your professional goals with something higher than yourself – it will give you the strength to keep walking even in stormy weather. By doing so, you will not stop even under extremely challenging circumstances. Always remember, true success is a state of mind, not material gains. It's about the spirit of success.

SELF-ASSESSMENT/ACTIONS

List three things about your physical fitness and health you are blessed with.

1. ____
2. ____
3. ____

List three things about your family and friends you are grateful for.

1. ____
2. ____
3. ____

List three things about your education and skills that make you feel lucky.

1. ____
2. ____
3. ____

List three things that make you privileged comparing to millions of underprivileged people around the world.

1. ____
2. ____
3. ____

List the three most important things in your life that are working.

1. ____

2. ____

3. ____

CHAPTER 4

BELIEVE IN YOURSELF

Self-confidence is one of the key things that separates a successful person from a failed one. Successful people are full of self-confidence whereas unsuccessful people suffer from poor self-esteem. The latter don't believe that they can represent themselves. It's a pity. It naturally raises a question: if you don't believe in yourself, why on earth should others believe in you? Like a mirror, your self-confidence will reflect others' confidence in you. When you have a poor self-image, others won't take you seriously. You suffer from an inferiority complex. It's a surefire way to mediocrity and self-sabotage. There may be several causes of your poor self-confidence. But lack of professional knowledge, skills and poor communication are the important ones. When you can diagnose your weaknesses, it is possible to take steps to address these. Due to a distorted view of success in society, many consider it to be a matter of genetics – only selective people possess the right genes for success. It's true that certain people may have genetic traits that may help them to gain certain skills faster.

However, practicing a craft over a long period of time consistently is the key to develop a skill. Only through practicing, can you acquire skills, improve them and become a world-class performer.

True success is making yourself better compared with the you of your past. You are not competing with others. In fact, you are competing with your past self by improving and updating your professional skills. In this, there is no limit. You can be as successful as you want to be. It's a self-directed inner process without any outer competition. You must get rid of the notion that someone else is responsible for your suffering and failures in life. Primarily, you are in sole control of your success or failure. You are responsible for creating your own life-story. Your actions should be dictated by the script you write, not others' opinions. Whatever life situation you are in, you can steer it to a better direction. You can initiate change merely by taking the decision to act. On the one hand, people with superior knowledge may live their lives far below their potential due to the lack of self-confidence and self-assertion. On the other, people with high self-confidence may advance their career even without proper education and work experience. It's about personal creativity, initiative and resourcefulness.

You can choose to become what you want in life. What separates a successful person from an average person is his level of positive self-perception and self-confidence. When you believe in yourself, you get access to inner resources that will help you to get things done. This helps you to become comfortable with yourself. It enables you to represent your boldest self to the world. This courage is a powerful source of positive energy. By using this, you can create extraordinary things in life. You can create an oasis in the desert. When you possess this energy, you can embrace reality without fear. It happens when one feels personally powerful. It's the result of believing in yourself and taking necessary preparations. Preparation builds up confidence. To achieve this feat, first you must discover your own innate abilities and use those to fuel your success in life. As success is an inner quest to overcome yourself, finding and using your own inner resources is very important. This will boost your self-respect.

DISCOVER THE GIFTS OF YOUR LIFE

All human beings are endowed with special abilities, gifts or talents. Everyone is good at something. Like a duck's natural ability to swim, a bird's natural ability to fly and a monkey's natural ability to climb a tree, every human being has unique natural strengths. It is the utmost duty of each person to discover his natural abilities. Unfortunately, the majority of people in the world don't know what they are truly capable of. As a result, they live a limited and average life far below their true potential. They die without ever knowing what they are truly capable of. What a tragedy! Each child and adult alike have different abilities or natural strengths. Everyone is naturally good at something. The role of teachers and family members is to discover in which area a child is talented in and give necessary support to nurture that strength. If they can do it properly, a student can become successful not only in a profession but also in life in general. Also, by considering the introversion or extroversion of a student's personality, teachers can help him in choosing the right career for him.

The main aim of schools is to control individual and group

behavior to ensure mass compliance. To this end, schools attempt to create standard students with the same quality and type of personality. They don't nurture individual needs and talents. Their aim is to make students fit into a society based on dominant social expectations. They also fail to give students creativity and problem-solving skills. As a result, though graduates may obtain certificates after successful completion of the school cycle, many don't get useful skills.

There are exceptions to this case too. The world-famous Finnish school education system is worth noting here. The most talented and qualified people are attracted to the teaching profession in Finland because of the government's higher investment in education. After their entry into the teacher education program at universities, through highly-competitive examinations, student teachers receive over five years of research-oriented education and training. Teachers, both inside the classroom and outside, assess individual strengths of students and support these strengths. They also give support to uplift those who are lagging behind to ensure that they also become successful as individuals as well as part of a team. The Finnish school education system helps students to find out and nurture their strengths. You can profitably use this lesson of the highly-successful Finnish school system for personal development. As individuals, the prime responsibility of your life is to discover your personal strengths and nurture these. You must attune your career and life plan with your true natural strengths or capabilities.

THE POWER OF A SONG

Abdul Gaffar Chowdhury, a Bangladeshi-born British writer, journalist and poet, is best known as the writer of the song *"Amar Bhaiyer Rokte Rangano Ekushey February"* in 1952. This was a moving tribute to Bengali youths who on 21st February laid down their lives to peacefully protect their linguistic rights against the will of the then Pakistani ruling class. Composed by Altaf Mahmud, the song inspired the Bengali nation to pursue the movement for provincial autonomy and to finally establish Bangladesh as an independent nation in 1971 after a bloody war. To promote linguistic and cultural diversity as well as multilingualism at international level, in 1999, UNESCO proposed to observe 21st February as the International Mother Language Day. Since 2000, the day has been observed throughout the world. If you can use your true gift in the right place and right time, it can become extremely powerful as we see from Chowdhury's example.

POSITION YOURSELF AT THE CENTER OF YOUR LIFE

For the sake of belonging to society, people usually surrender their individuality. In pursuit of socialization, they blindly copy others. They end up becoming mere shadows or echoes of others without any personal distinction. This is a serious blow to individual uniqueness and authenticity. Without becoming authentic and skilled, they cannot add value or contribute to society in a meaningful way. For success, you need to nurture and develop your spirit, being true to yourself. Don't be afraid of criticism. Critics will always criticize you, no matter how much good you do. You need to refuse to be sidelined or undermined by others in matters of your own life. You must respect yourself as a person under all circumstances. You must keep in mind that you don't need to surrender your individuality or personal choices in the name of friendship, acceptance or social norms. Remember that true friendship or community is possible only among equals. Those who fail to own their actions are not taken seriously. They become destined to live the life of a follower or a fan. If you lack in something, don't blame or undermine yourself. Rather, take specific actions to improve your skills and competence. The human mind is a powerful, magical tool. You should make the best use of it, not only to enrich yourself but also to help others. Don't let the social pressure for conformity derail you from fulfilling your true personal potential.

You must put yourself at the center of your life. Because of an inferiority complex, people rarely place themselves at the center of their life. For success, you must remain authentic to who you are. You must not fabricate or belittle any part of your identity. Diversity in personal, as well as broader, level is resourcefulness. Barack Obama was a popular U.S. president from 2009 to 2017. He did achieve historical feats as the first black president without surrendering his non-U.S. sounding family name "Obama". A person of multiple identities, he remained true to himself by respecting his African heritage as well. He inspired not only

American blacks or people of color but also people across Africa, Asia and Latin America. The lesson you can learn from him is that the "substance of character" of a person is much more important than a superficial form or trend. For real success, first, you must accept yourself as you are in color, appearance and physical characteristics. Then work on yourself to contribute better.

Generally, the whole storyline of a novel revolves around the central character of a hero or heroine. However powerful other characters may be, the protagonist is the most important of all. People with low self-esteem accept others' definition of them and assume a peripheral position in their own lives. They mimic and copy others. They fail to realize their true interests and individual strengths. As a result, they fail to use their inner power. You should not follow this path. You must become the protagonist of your own life.

To unlock your true potential, you must believe in yourself in the first place. You need to be adamant about it. Together with this, you must take action and discipline yourself to attract success in life. Many people mistakenly think of success as a destination or an event. In fact, it's an ongoing process. It requires commitment, action, discipline and grit. For success, you need to be true to yourself. Believing in yourself is the first step towards opening up a new world of possibilities. This requires strong willpower and endurance. By putting yourself at the center of your life, you can develop as a unique, productive and valuable member of society. To do this, you must step outside your comfort zone. By doing so, you will be able to create significance in your own right.

BE GOAL AND TASK-ORIENTED

In childhood, people get lots of encouragement from their parents and close family members. It is manifested in their educational and career choices. Parents' education and career have a strong influence on children's education and career choices. This influence leaves a permanent mark on the psyche when people become adults and old people themselves. Boys and girls follow their father and mother as role models. They get a sense of direction from their parents from an early age. That's why the children of athletes, doctors, businessmen and politicians etc., often choose the same profession as their parents. Other key influences include teachers and peers. Those who get career guidance at an early age find it easier to attain professional success. Those students who grow up in average rural families find it more difficult to make informed decisions about their education and career choices.

But in a well-functioning education system, the role of parents in educational and professional choices is less important. Teachers help students to make choices based on their personal interests and strengths. This is crucial for career success. In the schools and higher educational institutions of developed nations, students also have access to career advisors. This enables students to make informed career and life decisions. It gives them confidence in handling practical matters. In the absence of a good education system, students make career decisions based on guesswork. It's similar to throwing a stone into the darkness. It can only reach its destination by chance. Based on your personal interests and natural skills you can set your own career goals, prioritize and act. To reach your career goals, you must know where you are going.

LEARN TO SAY "NO"

People tend to go with the wind of social expectations and comply with social trends. Generally, they conform to public opinion to avoid social rejection and isolation. As many cannot imagine life outside society, they choose to fit in with social expectations. However, if you value your time and take yourself seriously, you cannot please all the people all the time. While you should be a decent and responsible member of society, with meaningful social interaction with others, you should also learn to say 'no' to timewasters. Your time is the most valuable resource in your life. You should not give away this vital resource to less important people for the sake of socialization. In whatever direction you choose in life, you will always find people who will criticize you or your actions unreasonably. Their criticism may say less about you and more about them, their personal failures, frustrations and miseries. You should not worry about such critics. If you follow other people's opinions about you, it is guaranteed that you will end up being a failure. If you try to focus on too many things at the same time, it may cause your downfall. I remember the story of The Greedy Spider, told by my paternal grandmother in my childhood.

There was a mother spider that was very fond of eating food. She never missed the chance of a feast. She ordered her children to inform her about any feast and take her there.

She connected herself with ropes and gave them to her children so that they could pull her to any feast. Things were going smoothly. As there were not many feasts in a day or a week, there was initially no problem with pulling the ropes. One day, something went seriously wrong. All the spider's children pulled their ropes from different directions at the same time to take her to feasts. The greedy spider died of suffocation.

If you don't care about your own goals, who else is going to? Avoid chronically unhappy and toxic people. They may infect you with their negative attitude. Use your time selectively and judiciously. Like a gardener, you should ruthlessly remove weeds from your garden to allow healthy conditions for flowers to grow. When you plant your seeds, only flowers should bloom, nothing else. First and foremost, you should please yourself instead of pleasing others. In the long run, you will see the positive results of such crucial actions. It doesn't matter what goal you pursue in life, you will be criticized in one way or another. You should claim your individuality so that you can ignore habitual critics. You must learn to say "no" to such people. It will save you time that you can invest in further personal development for moving ahead in life. Bear in mind that you cannot always please everyone. So, stop the notion that you must please everyone.

BE A READER

The average adult seldom reads to learn after getting their diplomas. Knowledge earned from educational institutions is mostly academic and impractical in many parts of the world. Obtaining mere certificates doesn't necessarily mean one is attaining skills or competence. Reading books regularly builds people's mental power. It enables you to connect disparate ideas to create something completely new and original. You must be a good reader in order to live a successful life. Books are your true friends. At one stage of your life, a close friend may betray you. But books will never do that. Building up a regular reading habit will make you a knowledgeable, confident and strong-willed person. The majority of the world's richest and most successful people are good readers. You can build up your reading habit by borrowing books from libraries or buying books from bookstores. Reading books will provide you with new ideas that can enrich you as a person. This can also add value in your profession and can help you create a fortune. Through books, you can gain knowledge and wisdom of different eras of human history. Plutarch related the reading of books to authentic living. If you read the right kind of books, these will broaden your horizon and herald a new era of possibility. But in this digital age, people are obsessed with getting instant news feeds from social media without checking the facts. In this context, reading books is the only way to make the distinction between propaganda and truth.

By reading books, you can separate yourself from the crowd. This will help you to enrich your intellectual capacity. It can help you to become an expert or industry leader in a chosen field. The more you read books, the more knowledgeable and competitive you will become. You will get new ideas and perspectives that will help sharpen your career skills.

Born into a farming family, Abraham Lincoln later became the sixteenth President of the U.S.A. He was an avid reader of books. His *Emancipation Proclamation* of 1863 paved the way for the ending slavery in the U.S.

In addition to his knowledge of core teachings of the world's major and minor religions, Mahatma Gandhi also came across Western writers whose powerful ideas sparked fires in his mind. He put those ideas into action and became one of the greatest souls of human history.

Jawaharlal Nehru, the first prime minister and one of the architects of modern India, was an avid reader and widely-published writer. Nehru was one of the initiators of the Non-Aligned Movement (NAM), the largest organization after the United Nations. It was established in 1961 to keep nations of the world outside the sphere of influence of the two Cold War military blocs.

In May 2016, U.S. President Barak Obama hosted a State Dinner for Nordic leaders: Danish Prime Minister Lars Lokke Rasmussen, Finnish President Sauli Niinistö, Icelandic Prime Minister Sigurdur Ingi Johansson, Norwegian Prime Minister Erna Solberg and Swedish Prime Minister Stefan Lofven. In the dinner speech, as seen and heard in a video of The Obama White House, Obama expressed his tribute to Danish philosopher N.F.S. Grundtvig and the progressive democratic values of Nordic nations on equality, justice and active citizenship. He acknowledged the "ripples of hope" of Grundtvig's powerful idea of the Folk High School that

Reading contributes to the increase of earning power as well. The world's well-known billionaires such as Jeff Bezos, Bill Gates, Warren Buffet, Mark Zuckerberg, Elon Musk and Oprah Winfrey are ardent readers of books. They spend time on reading every day despite extremely busy schedules.

DO YOUR BEST

It's easy to blame others for things that go wrong. However, it requires courage to take individual responsibility instead of running away from a problem. By running away from a problem, you cannot escape from it. Over time, it comes back bigger in size and more difficult to handle. You have to face the reality on the face of it. Your act of courage will help you to project yourself as a credible person. You don't need to wait for others to solve your problems. You can overcome problems by yourself. To find out who you are at the core is a million Euro question. When you discover the answer, you will be a different person. Then, you will have better self-understanding and clarity of purpose. Self-examination can be a daunting task. When you take ownership of your thinking and actions, you are best placed to create real success. You must keep yourself prepared all the time for taking up challenges. This concentration will help you to reap the fruits of your labor in the future. It will build up inner strength and remove anxiety and fear. In this state, you will not react to circumstances any more. Rather, you will proactively embrace progress and change.

When you do your best and continue to improve knowledge and skills, you will have no regrets about your past. You will be at peace with yourself. You will not need any outside validation. You will feel that you are the master of your own fate. It's a journey from within; a journey of self-discovery. Even if the whole world rejects or ridicules you, you will remain calm and confident about yourself. It's a journey of courage and defying the odds. It requires that you go the extra mile. You must read more, ask more questions, work more, learn more and grow more. It's undoubtedly a painstaking process. But the fruits of this accomplishment will be sweet indeed.

VISUALIZE YOURSELF AS A WINNER

When you know your passion, discover your gifts and talents in life and can set your professional goals, you are on the right track for success. In order to reach your goal, thinking positively and setting a goal are not enough. You must create a "mental blueprint" for success in your subconscious mind. This self-image can rapidly prepare you for success. It's the result of positive mental attitude. When you can visualize, feel and act as a successful person, you can get rid of limiting self-perception. This will imbue confidence in yourself to achieve any goal in life. This can transform your life from failure to success.

You must align your actions with your self-image. This will increase your self-confidence. You will feel at ease with yourself. To guide your life in this direction, surround yourself with the right books, pictures and ideas of successful people in your personal space. This will create their presence in your life as if you are in conversation with them in reality. This presence is very powerful. Living in the right kind of environment gives you a feeling that you are already in the company of winners. When you reach this state, you are halfway towards your success. All you have to do is become true to yourself and your passion. You must take consistent and disciplined actions. This will work as a foundation towards your success. Though it may require investment of much time and energy, it will pay off handsomely in the long run.

You can make your knowledge better organized by visualizing the path of your success. This is crucial for better performance. The more you practice, the more skilled you become with visualization. When you can single-mindedly visualize and work on your dream, you remove fear from your mind. In this charged mental state, you can achieve any goal.

I'm sure that you remember Kylian Mbappe, the French teenage footballer and the hero of the FIFA World Cup final 2018, held in Russia. A boy from a poor Paris suburb, he scored a goal against Croatia in the final helping the French squad to win the World Cup. He became the second teenager after football legend Pele to score in a World Cup final. He comes from an immigrant background: his father originated from Cameroon and mother from Algeria. Growing up with a passion for football, he spent most of his time practicing the game. His dream was to become a football superstar. As a fan of football star Cristiano Ronaldo, he adorned his bedroom with posters of his idol. By visualizing and doing relentless practice, he himself became a megastar of world football. He did this by surpassing his idol, Ronaldo, as well as other star players. In fact, he surpassed his own dream.

UNDERSTAND SITUATIONS

It's great to have an idealistic view of the world. But you must protect yourself in the first place. Believing in others doesn't mean that you shouldn't be cautious. Cunning and manipulative persons, as well as psychopaths, are also out there. They just look like other humans. There is no special mark on their faces so that you can identify and stay away from them. They are each like a wolf in sheep's clothing. They are dangerous. They can devastate you emotionally. Though the number of such people is very small in all societies, they can damage your trust in people. In traditional cultures, seniority in birth order and social relations attracts respect. But some people use their cultural position to take advantage of others. Though you can be deferential to others, you should never undermine yourself. Mentally, you should be big enough that nobody can take advantage of you or undermine you. It's not a matter of ego but of principle. You must protect yourself from bullies who don't possess a "working conscience". If you cannot protect yourself, nobody is going to protect you. Without protecting yourself, you cannot realize your ideals or help others. So, instead of passively accepting yourself as a lackey, claim your individuality by employing all means. Be your truest friend. In time, with the right actions, you can make yourself a valuable and respected person.

To protect yourself and lead a life of success, you must diagnose and understand a problem accurately. This will help you to figure out an appropriate solution based on your needs. You must develop a far-sighted vision of the world. Instead of blaming others, you must develop skills and insights to develop yourself. When someone stoops low, you should not take it personally. It's the problem of the other person, not yours. You should ignore the mean act and take the higher ground. It's the best revenge you can take against an unethical, mean or opportunist person.

The lessons of this chapter will help you to get a broader perspective on life. They will increase your confidence in yourself. They will motivate you to leave your painful past behind and move forward in your quest for achievement. Believing yourself is the first step towards success.

SELF-ASSESSMENT/ACTIONS

List three characteristics that best describe you as a person.

1. ____

2. ____

3. ____

List three special abilities, talents or gifts you possess but have not utilized yet.

1. ____

2. ____

3. ____

List three dream careers in order of priority that you truly want to pursue.

1. ____

2. ____

3. ____

List three things that hold you back from pursuing your dream career.

1. ____

2. ____

3. ____

List three actions you must take to bring faith in yourself.

1. ____

2. ____

3. ____

CHAPTER 5

FOLLOW YOUR PASSION

Every person is naturally endowed with special gifts in life. People are naturally good at something. Because of the popular trend towards conformity to social expectations, the vast majority of people fail to value their true passions. As a result, they fail to discover their personal qualities and nurture them. They spend most of their time fulfilling basic needs and responding to life circumstances. For them, following their own passions is a luxury they cannot afford. They fail to understand that the struggle for survival should not stop you pursing your own dreams.

Curiosity and imagination are enough to live the life of your dreams. They help people to realize their goals. People who have limiting beliefs about themselves cannot fulfill their true potential in life. That's why even after receiving opportunities, some people cannot use them successfully. They lack the inner urge and strong motivation. Because of this, there is a proverb, "You can take a horse to water, but you can't make it drink." Without understanding their passion and true potential, people prefer to imitate or copy others. Unfortunately, the vast majority of people of the world fall into this category. Indeed, it's a tragic waste of human potential.

To walk a higher road in life, you have to get rid of limiting beliefs. When you free yourself of limiting beliefs, you can live a life of true passion. It happens when you are not afraid to be different from others. This requires that you believe in your own dream. Inner desire and passion work as fuel for creating magic in life. People wish for a long life for their nearest and dearest. But gaining a long life should not be the primary aim of people. They should focus on making their lives useful and full of contribution to others. Jean Jacques Rousseau considered the importance of life to be based on one's sense of living instead of longevity by years. But most people live life without a sense of living. They live a passive life and count it quantitatively. Only a minority have a true sense of living in this world or effective living. Many don't make active choices in life or realise their power to choose. They live a mechanistic life. Some live their life devoid of any purpose as if they are the walking dead. Social conformity often destroys their potential and forces them to live an average life. But problems or impediments in life are not final or permanent. With strong determination and hard work, you can remove hurdles and make yourself an effective and successful person.

PASSION LEADS TO SUCCESS

Passion generates intense desire that helps in creating success in life. It is useful for pursuing a life of purpose. To make your dream a reality, you must pursue it with imagination, intense feeling and dedication. These will help you to create a roadmap for the future with a sense of inner direction. Everyone has dreams. However, the majority of people fail to create their career or life blueprint based on their dreams. Blind imitation of others destroys their individual dreams. As they don't create a career or life plan with a deadline, their wishes remain wishes only. To become successful, you have to have curiosity as well as an intense passion for achieving your dream. As adult brains are loaded with everyday problems, many lose their imagination in the face of reality. Children are imaginative, curious and playful about the surrounding world. They are open to experimentation. You must believe in your dreams with the same faith and conviction as a child. If you wholeheartedly invest your time, energy and money in achieving an important goal, some people may say that you are acting like a child. Take such an insult as a badge of honor. When people begin to attack you, you should know that you are on the right path. When you walk on the right path, you will invariably be attacked by small minds. You don't need to react to them. If you do so, you will engage in their sinister games. Let them do their job and pursue your own path. Your success should speak louder than your words. It is said that when the sun rises, everybody notices it.

Passion can help people create a new purpose of life. It's a powerful force for making sense of life, despite serious hurdles in achieving success. World-famous innovators such as Microsoft's main founder, Bill Gates, and its current

CEO, Satya Nadella, co-founder of Apple Steve Jobs, Google's current CEO Sundar Pichai, and Ali Baba Group's co-founder Jack Ma, all share a common quality. Each of them advanced their career and became a symbol of world-class professional success because of their passion for their chosen work. They followed their passion and remained true to themselves. On their way to success, all of them faced many ups and downs. However, they were able to overcome them because of their love and commitment to their career.

Bengali educationist and social reformer Ishwar Chandra Vidyasagar lived his life in the 19th century. He was a key figure of the Bengali renaissance. In recognition of this polymath's wide-ranging knowledge, he was awarded the title "*Biddyasagar*" or Ocean of Knowledge. Even today, he is highly regarded in Bangladesh and the Indian state of West Bengal. Vidyasagar was born in a poor family. From his childhood, he had a passion for knowledge. It is legendary that as he could not afford gas lamps at home, he studied beneath a streetlight.

Kazi Nazrul Islam is the national poet of Bangladesh. Because of his vocal activism for political and social justice through poems as well lyrics, he is popularly known as the "Rebel Poet." He had lived a childhood of poverty. But poverty could not stop him from pursing his passion for learning and artistic pursuits. He continued to support his dream sometimes by working as a cook, a tea stall boy and sometimes as a soldier of the British Indian Army.

Narendra Modi, the prime minister of India was born in a disadvantaged social group. In his childhood, he used to sell tea with his father in a small town. His self-trust and passion for politics helped him to overcome all class and cultural barriers to success. He was re-elected as the prime minister of India after his party's landslide victory in the 2019 general election.

PURSUE YOUR OWN DREAMS

Abdus Sattar Dulal is a pioneer of the disabled people's rights movement in Bangladesh and internationally and the executive director of *Bangladesh Protibandhi Kallyan Somity (BPKS)*. At the age of 15, he fell from a tree and survived after forty-two days in a coma. After that, he became confined to a wheelchair. He overcame physical and social hurdles through the sheer power of his dream. He served as the World Counselor at Disabled People's International (DPI). In 2012, he was awarded the honor of "Disability Rights Champion" by the UN. With his concept of "Persons with Disabilities Self-Initiative to Development" (PSID) he has so far organized and trained thousands of disabled people of Bangladesh through specialist training organizations. He has brought about a new confidence in them to take charge of their lives through the development of skills and entrepreneurship. I have seen for myself with my own eyes the sparks of self-confidence in disabled people who have received training and support from BPKS. They were

When people have their own dream or calling, they make greater efforts to achieve it. They don't hesitate to sacrifice anything to fulfill that dream. As they have a compelling reason to succeed in life, they feel that they have nothing to lose. When one's dream is connected to something bigger and greater than oneself – such as family, community, humanity or God – people can defy all odds. They simply go for what they want to achieve. Strong motivation pulls them to achieve miracles. You must have a dream to make it a reality. People who do not see the inner passion of a dreamer, may invariably consider him queer, irrational or unrealistic. But inner passion is a fire that can change the world. James Allen considered dreams as the seedlings of realities. Dreams pull people forward to reach their goals.

Through experiments, you can figure out what strategy works for you. Remember that you are a work-in-progress. You have to both love yourself and what you do. You must create your uniqueness through development of professional skills and competence. Uniqueness in dreams, personality and actions will create a unique you. This is how stars and megastars are born. To pursue a life of success and fulfillment, you must dare to dream in the first place. A dream with vision, action and discipline can make your fears irrelevant. It will make you bold enough to take on new challenges. When you can pursue your goals without fear, no hurdles can stop you.

CONNECT GOALS TO THE HIGHER PURPOSE OF LIFE

In life, you should have the courage to dream big, act big and achieve big. When you can set higher targets and higher standards for yourself, you can achieve anything. When you have a higher purpose in life, together with a sense of self-worth and self-confidence, you will not be overtaken by majority trends or deterred from your goals by temporary setbacks. You will be strongly motivated to pursue your goals no matter what. No hurdle will be big enough to stop you. By setting higher goals for serving community and humanity, Florence Nightingale, Henry Dunant and Fridtjof Nansen changed the face of modern nursing, humanitarian work and refugee rights.

What motivated such great souls to contribute to change the world in a better direction? Altruism. It made them rise above others to dedicate their lives in the service of suffering humanity. Florence Nightingale, an English social reformer known as "The Lady with the Lamp", organized care of wounded soldiers with a team of nurses and Catholic nuns during the Crimean War in the 1850s. She found deep meaning in professionally nursing the sick and becoming the founder of modern nursing.

Henry Dunant, a Swiss businessman and social activist, was moved by the human suffering during the Battle of Solferino in Italy in 1859. To help injured and sick soldiers, he built makeshift hospitals with the help of others. His ideas paved the way for the creation of the *Geneva Convention*, on international law for the protection of victims of armed conflicts. For his role in establishing the International Red Cross and Geneva Convention, he was awarded the first Nobel Peace Prize in 1901.

Fridtjof Nansen, a Norwegian explorer, scientist, diplomat and humanitarian is known for his pioneering work on refugee rights. He devised a document for stateless persons that later became known as the "Nansen passport". He was awarded the Nobel Peace Prize in 1922.

STAY FOCUSED

To summon positive mental energy for success, you need to take control of your mind. When you have a clear purpose, faith in yourself and focused action, these will attract success into your life. The majority of people who want to become successful, have too broad a focus. As a result, they get overwhelmed with the enormity of the task at hand. They ultimately give up on their goals. However, when your focus is narrowed down and concentrated, it becomes easy to implement. Microsoft, Google, CNN, Apple, Amazon, Alibaba and Kone each focus on a single sector or aligned industry (Windows program, search engine, 24-hour TV news channel, iPhone, books, consumer websites, and elevators). Because of their focused action, they have emerged as unique companies in the world, virtually without competition. Had the focus of those companies been too broad, they might have been lost in mass competition. At an individual level too, the same truth is applicable. A single area of concentrated focus brings concrete results. By doing so, you can create a name that will be remembered in the industry you are working in.

Abdul Sattar Edhi, a Pakistani philanthropist, humanitarian and the founder of the Edhi Foundation, had compassion for vulnerable and helpless people. His childhood experience of hardships and challenges made him a thoughtful person with a caring heart. He extended this love to other people in need. Today, his foundation runs homeless shelters, animal shelters, hospitals, an ambulance service, orphanages and educational services across Pakistan. It was his single-minded focus on helping the poor and vulnerable that made him well-known as a philanthropist across Pakistan and the world.

For success, you must single-mindedly focus on one area of action. After achieving one goal, you can then move on to the next. This will help you with getting things done. Your focus should enable you to nurture existing skills, help you to develop new skills and to become a lifelong learner to professionally take yourself to the next level. If the task is too big, you must divide it into smaller pieces to make it executable. It's the right preparation to enable you to take on the challenges of life. Doing your homework and relentless preparation will set you apart from the rest. Only by going out of your comfort zone and carrying out your actions relentlessly, can you attain your goal. Your focused and consistent action will remove self-doubt, fear and worries and imbue self-confidence.

FIND A ROLE MODEL

Finding a role model and emulating him or her will accelerate your success. Once you are sure about the merits of your goal and get motivated to pursue it, lessons from a role model can help you tremendously. As schools, and society in general, fail to provide people with lessons on career and life skills, reading books may provide you with valuable insights of successful people past and present. You also need to befriend successful people and adopt their qualities in your life. We are living in an exciting time. Mobile Internet is changing the world fast. What seemed even impossible to think about in the 1980s has become a reality now. When I came to Finland from Bangladesh as an international student in 1996, it was the era of snail mail. It took two to four weeks for a handwritten letter to travel from one country to another. Landline phone quality was poor. A call to Bangladesh had to go through a telephone exchange. Finnish Nokia and Swedish Ericsson mobile sets were not yet widely available. Over a period of two decades, the situation has changed dramatically. Even a village boy from Bangladesh now has access to mobile Internet. Now we live in a digitally-connected world. You have to use the power of technology to improve your career and life.

By following a role model in your specific field of interest or industry, you can strive for success at an accelerated speed. It does not matter whether you are an athlete, singer, officer, office worker, professional, businessman or whatever. There are national and global role models for you to follow in your niche. You must find the right role models to emulate. You can access their ideas, knowledge and expertise from their books, videos or podcasts. In this digital age, you will be able to learn from them without the hurdles of middlemen or gatekeepers. By using free or cheap digital tools, you can pursue your goals independently. In this age of democratic possibility, you can achieve skills without the need to invest a fortune. To become a leader, you must follow a leader. The worldwide rise of indie artists, stars and writers is a manifestation of this digital revolution. You can use the power of digital media to boost your career. By following the right role model and working on yourself, you can create your own fortune.

Originally a self-published e-book of E.L. James, *Fifty Shades of Grey*, later became the first instalment in the *Fifty Shades Trilogy* from Vintage Books, a subdivision of Random House. It sold millions of copies around the world and topped the best-seller charts, surpassing J.K. Rowling's *Harry Potter*. It has been translated into many different languages.

Amish Tripathi, a banker turned writer, is a literary superstar of India. He is well known for his books in the Shiva Trilogy. After his manuscript was repeatedly rejected by publishers, he self-published his first book, *The Immortals of Meluha*. After that, he never looked back. His name was included in Forbes' 2018 top 100 celebrities in India (based on their wealth) such as Salman Khan, Virat Kohli and Akshay Kumar.

Gangnam Style, the lead single song released by South Korean musician Psy, became the first YouTube video that hit record views in the world in 2012. It remains one of the most viewed videos in YouTube's history.

Ashraful Alam Saeed, popularly known as *Hero Alam* of Bogra, Bangladesh, is a well-known music video model, actor and social media sensation. An unlikely hero or star in the Bangladeshi context because of his dark skin color, appearance, local accent and below high school education, he has risen to prominence from a humble background through his burning desire. He became famous through the power of social media. He has often faced widespread online trolling and been a popular subject of memes. He was inspired by CD cover pictures of stars from his pre-celebrity life.

You can gather ideas from people of the past and present by reading their books. Based on this knowledge, you can figure out a suitable path for yourself. You can take the decision according to your own personality traits, interests and skills. By doing so, you can create a brand-new direction for your life. This requires that you master the craft of your choice with actions, consistency and discipline. It is similar to declaring the independence of your spirit – the most important step towards realizing your dreams. This will make you feel good about yourself. In this digital age, there is no doorkeeper or middleman between you and your dreams. If you are determined, nothing can thwart you from achieving goals. With the help of digital tools, you can reach your potential. All you need is to act on your dream. There is no limit to what you can achieve. You can achieve as much as you can imagine. Whatever you need for massive success is in your own hands. In fact, it is right at your fingertips. You can achieve your goals in a much shorter period than any other era of human history. If you want to get tons of inspiration on how to reach out to the world through social media, you can follow the leading global social media influencers such as Guy Kawasaki, Gary Vaynerchuk, Tim Ferris, Neil Patel and Jeff Bullas among others.

SELF-ASSESSMENT/ACTIONS

List three dreams you have always wanted to pursue.

1. ____

2. ____

3. ____

List three things in life that excite and energize you.

1. ____

2. ____

3. ____

List three things you are good at or that set you apart from others.

1. ____

2. ____

3. ____

List three values/higher purposes that make sense of your life.

1. ____

2. ____

3. ____

List three people that you admire as role models.

1. ____

2. ____

3. ____

List the three most important achievements in your life.

1. ____

2. ____

3. ____

CHAPTER 6

DESIGN YOUR DREAM CAREER

Once you know your true passion and dream, it's time to design a life that will work for you. You must articulate your thinking and create a clear set of goals. One key difference between an animal and a human being is that humans can plan ahead. Animals go for instant gratification. But humans are capable of planning ahead and following it through. One key purpose of human life is to make sense of it. It is about transforming yourself from a state of "imperfection" to "perfection." When you know your unique strengths and are able to nurture them, you can create a new life. To live such a life, you need to set your career goals. If you live life with a clear mission and vision, you will not regret it later.

Most people in the world copy others without defining their goals and life purpose. Their "follower mentality" reflects little of their true interests and personal strengths. In many countries of the world, students wish to become doctors, engineers, police officers, army officers, Foreign Service officers, etc., due to the social value of these professions, rather than for any genuine personal interest. The ultimate goal of the education system in many societies is to create regular employees for general positions, rather than people with specialized skills. Those who can manage to catch the golden deer of prestigious positions, are considered successful. Others are considered failures. Whether a person carries out his responsibilities with passion or not, is not taken into consideration. This is the mindset of mediocrity.

It is tragic to find that in certain circumstances, there is hardly any qualitative difference between a university-educated person and an illiterate person in terms of practical skills. It is difficult to find any substantial difference between them except for the possession of certificates and dressing in a certain way. Apparently, education is used as a filter to separate the privileged from the common people, rather than making them more skilled. In Bangladesh, the trademark difference between an educated and an uneducated man is that the former feels ashamed to wear traditional *lungi* outside their home. They also feel uncomfortable doing manual labor. The ultimate purpose of education is to create a large number of office clerks, in addition to a handful of officers. Education hardly instills curiosity, skills and self-initiative among educated people. This is evident in many parts of the world and in many post-colonial societies of Asia and Africa in particular. High youth unemployment, the rise of drug abuse and youth violence are a manifestation of weaknesses within the existing education systems. To lead an effective life, you must design a specific career plan with short-, medium- and long-term goals. It is of utmost importance that you implement this plan with action.

SET PERSONALIZED GOALS

Generally, individuals make education, career and life decisions by following others, or more precisely, following popular trends. These are seldom based on their true passions. They are largely mechanistic. As people don't plan a career that is connected to a deeply-felt inner urge, millions of people around the world suffer from a lack of motivation. Instead of taking ownership of their work, they follow others and react to circumstances. The majority dislike, and many hate, their work. They are always in crisis management mode in their career. The failure to set personalized goals lowers their motivation and productivity at work. People become unhappy in their career. This has negative implications for the individual's workplace environment, family and social relations. Public, private and non-governmental organizations around the world lose billions of euros each year because of this problem. If you are suffering from the same difficulty, it's high time for you to take steps to fix it.

As an initial step, you must identify what you really want to do, organize your ideas and set your personalized goals within an actionable timeframe. Then you can make a practical roadmap to reach your goals. First of all, you have to find a career that truly suits your passions and natural capabilities. We all have plenty of thoughts and ideas sitting idly in our brains. Though important, we seldom use them. Once you get a new idea, write it down. Otherwise, you may lose the idea. Among your many ideas, you can finalize goals based on your priorities in life. Once you finalize your goals through this filtering process, it will allow you to concentrate energy in a focused way. Everybody doesn't necessarily need to pursue higher education or academic degrees, which are often just a status symbol. Only a small percentage of people can use their education successfully. Those who fail to go through highly-competitive examinations, become frustrated. If you feel good pursuing technical and vocational education, you should pursue it without looking for an academic degree. It will make you a skilled person. As competition for skilled jobs is less, you can easily get a job at the end of your education. If you don't want to do a traditional job working for someone else, you can become an entrepreneur. Overall, you should choose an education and career that truly energizes you and gives you skills. As soon as you can unlearn that career is a matter of status, it's better for you.

In developing, as well as in developed nations, there is a bias towards academic education. After pursuing higher education, millions of people compete with each other to secure public and private sector jobs. Unable to secure a dream job, most people choose a career that has nothing to do with their educational degree. A large group of people end up being unemployed. Highly-educated people from developing countries migrate to the developed nations of North America, Europe and Oceania. In the new environment, a vast majority of them end up taking odd jobs that don't suit their educational level. Linguistic barriers, skill gaps and lack of willingness to update skills are some of the reasons for this. We are living in a paradoxical world. On the one hand, there is rising unemployment among the educated people. On the other, there is a shortage of technically-skilled people in certain sectors. People don't need a university degree to fill many of these jobs: a college degree or technical and vocational training is enough to qualify. For example, many nations need more and more nurses, drivers, welders, plumbers, electricians, mechanics, counseling professionals, social and healthcare professionals, radiographers and medical laboratory technicians. It is important that you choose a profession that you are passionate about as well as considering your employment prospects. When you keep in mind employability or marketability of your skill, it enables you to reach your goals successfully.

Goal setting is the first step you can take to make your dream a reality. It's like a mission statement that reflects your blueprint. You can use SWOT Analysis (strengths, weaknesses, opportunities and threats) to set your personalized goals. If you implement multiple goals at the same time, you may get disoriented due to the enormity of the task. However, if you do one thing at a time, the task will be much easier to carry out. If you divide your tasks into smaller pieces, you can implement those easily in a step-by-step manner. When you implement one goal at a time with focused energy, you will be more effective in achieving your outcome. It is important that your goal should be in alignment with your true priorities and broader life goals. Once your career goals are set, let your family and friends know. Making them public will push you on. It will serve as an outer pressure to act on your stated goals.

GET PRIORITIES RIGHT

Setting your career goals is all about getting your professional priorities right. You should prioritize things according to what matters to you most. It is good to remember that you are not competing with anyone else but trying to tap into your personal resources. Many people around the world have misplaced priorities in career, family and life. When priorities are wrong, results are bound to be disappointing. For success, setting the right priorities is a must. You need to get rid of the urgency trap in order to focus on the most important things in your life. Action is the bridge between the destination and where you stand now. The most successful people in the world are successful because they use their time effectively and prioritize their goals. It is important that you use most of your time to achieve your career goals.

But millions of people fail to prioritize their actions. They fail to recognize that everything doesn't have equal value or return. They confuse activities for results. To build a life of purpose, you must take charge of your life. It is a serious undertaking that requires self-reflection. Your family members and teachers may help you with feedback or giving perspective on this. You have to reduce unproductive social contacts and less productive activities in order to give more time to important people and activities. As friends can drain or add to your productivity, you must be selective in choosing them. You need to become friends with people who either inspire or add value in your life. Stay away from chronically unhappy people and complainers for they will infect your mind with negative thoughts. My suggestion may appear selfish to you. But when you distance yourself from negative people and spend most of your time with positive ones, you will see the results for yourself. You won't regret it. Don't wait for the perfect moment to come in order to take the right course. You should set your priorities right away. Choose the right people in your life and act now to become successful. Don't leave it until tomorrow. Act today!

To become successful, it is imperative that you focus on high-value tasks over low-value ones. You will need to develop knowledge and skills that will fuel extraordinary career success. You should figure out two or three major skills that will maximize your value in the marketplace. You should start with one skill at a time. When you master one, you can move to master another. You must invest time, money and energy for skills development as this will lead you to rapid career progression. When you are able to do this, you will be surprised to see the quality of the outcome. What you need is to find out and commit to your true priorities.

MAKE THE DECISION

Procrastination is a serious hurdle in the way of people's success. Everybody wants to be successful in life. But only a small group of people can actually be successful in fulfilling their dreams. Why? Generally, people look for comfort and stability. They prefer to delay today's tasks until tomorrow and tomorrow's work until the day after tomorrow. After a while, they discover that they have a huge of pile of work waiting to be done. It looks so big that it is difficult to even start carrying out the task. To get rid of this vicious cycle of procrastination, you must make the decision to act on your dreams.

Making the decision and implementing it plays a crucial role in achieving a goal. Once the decision is made, you have to execute it. Otherwise, what's the difference between taking a decision and not taking it? If you don't implement a decision after taking it, you lose credibility with yourself. Sometimes, a big problem, too heavy-to-bear pain or embarrassment pushes people into making a decision. It pushes them to act decisively.

Many world-class successful people changed their lives simply by taking the decision to become successful in the face of humiliating experiences. They could not take unbearable conditions any more. Decision-making is an extremely powerful tool for success. It has the power to turn things around. You should involve your emotions in implementing your decisions. This will push you to get rid of the unwanted situation and pull you to achieve your goals. When you can use your emotions for career and life success, you will never look back. Whether or not you are in a sorry state, make a decision to chart a new path of career and life success. Let your nearest and dearest know about your decision so that you have a reason to follow through with it.

ALIGN YOUR GOALS WITH YOUR LIFE PURPOSE

It is extremely important that your career goals should correspond to your value system and broader life goals. If you set a goal that contradicts your values, beliefs and life goals, you will sacrifice your peace of mind. Even if you become rich and successful, you will not be happy. What's the value of such success? Is life only about hoarding money and increasing influence? Of course not. If you spend your life only on money and influence without developing a value system, you will be forced to engage in a battle with your own mind. It means you will always face an inner crisis. You will be in a constant crisis management mode, without a way out. Can there be anything worse than this? To solve this problem, you must set your career goals in alignment with your true passion, value system and life goals. You should make sure that your career goals fit with the broader purpose of your life. Whatever your career goals are, your reasons for achieving those are crucially important.

If you can relate your career goals to your own survival, dignity and the future of your family, you will be highly motivated to take action. You can also relate this to contributing to your community or broader humanity. If you don't connect it with something higher than yourself, an occasional barrier or disappointment may derail you. To reach your goals, you need a strong drive to carry on your duties. Many people pursue their career success based on immediate goals without connecting these to their purpose of life. As a result, when they face sudden obstacles or pains along the way, they easily get dissuaded from their goals. You must connect your goals with your higher purpose in life so that you have reasons to stick to your goals no matter what. You can endure extreme pains and survive. This higher purpose of life can vary from individual to individual. This can be family, community, humanity, God, or important unfinished tasks.

SET DEADLINES FOR ACHIEVING GOALS

After you set your goals, the most important action is to set a specific timeframe within which to achieve them. Setting goals without a specific deadline may mean they are nothing more than wishful thinking. Without a clear timeframe, you may end up procrastinating. Some career goals are short-term and some are long-term. If you want to develop a new skill, you must develop a new habit. A new habit can be developed by spending a certain amount of time in daily practice towards a specific goal over a set time period. The longer you practice, the stronger the new habit or skill you can develop. To ensure progress, you must measure your daily, weekly, monthly and yearly progress. To achieve a long-term or higher-level goal, you can set a three-year, five-year and even a ten-year plan. If you intend to become a competitive athlete, you might set a two-year goal to become a national champion and a three-year goal to become an Olympic champion. If you intend to become a world-class expert in any craft or field, you may take three, five or even ten years to reach that goal. You can set similar time-bound goals to realize your targets for improving family relationship, personal effectiveness, interpersonal communication and so on.

Whether you are a student, employed person, unemployed person or an expert, you must allocate time for daily practice towards achieving your goal. You should focus on one thing at a time. Pursuing too many goals at the same time may make you lose focus and derail you. To develop a new skill, in the beginning you have to allocate at least one to two hours for practice every day. However, ideally, four to five hours of practice every day will help to give you momentum. You must stick to your daily routine no matter what. If you are achieving extraordinary feats in your career within a short time, it will encourage you to spend more hours every day. When you are able to do this for an extended period of time on a regular basis, it will separate you from others. You will become a remarkable person with a higher level of professional knowledge and skills. Once you reach a goal, it will strongly motivate you to take up the next goal… and then, the next.

If you want to take your career to new heights, you must always update your professional skills. You must commit to your goal and take action. You must finish your task within a deadline. Action is the mother of all fortunes. You have to make yourself accountable: you have to invest the necessary time, money and energy to reach your goals. You have to constantly work on yourself and keep track of your progress. That's why you need to create milestones or deliverables with specific timeframes. If a court order is not backed up with strong force, do you think people would take it seriously? Certainly not. Similarly, if you don't follow through your plan, you will not be able to translate your goals into reality. You have to take full responsibility for achieving your targets. To achieve your goal, you must stick to your actions no matter what. Results speak louder than words.

SELF-ASSESSMENT/ACTIONS

List the three most important career goals you want to pursue.

1. ____

2. ____

3. ____

In what way do your career goals suit your life goals?

1. ____

2. ____

3. ____

List three tasks/actions that will accelerate your career success.

1. ____

2. ____

3. ____

List three goals you want to achieve in one, three and five years.

1. ____

2. ____

3. ____

List three deliverables in one, three and five years.

1. ____

2. ____

3. ____

CHAPTER 7

TAKE MASSIVE ACTION

In this world, the majority of people cannot use their career potential. There are millions of unemployed people around the world, which is a loss of valuable human energy both for these people and society in general. A large proportion of those who are in work remain poorly motivated. As a result, productivity suffers. Most of these people are generally average or possess less knowledge and skills. Organizations remain less productive and are ineffective as a result. Lack of professional development, lack of personal loyalty, favoritism and factionalism have become prominent features of workplace culture in many countries. The result is lots of activity but with very few results. Government offices in many developing countries are examples of such organizational ineffectiveness. If you want to eliminate such a situation, you need to improve your specialized knowledge and skills. Only when you add distinct value to an industry, will you get a natural edge over others. In order to achieve massive success, you must take massive action.

Many people overrate the value of talent. They give less importance to preparation. When a person takes the right preparations, he can be successful irrespective of his talent. With regular practice, you can become valuable in your industry. You may add so much value that others may not consider you as their competitor. With regular practice, you can make competition irrelevant; you can become irreplaceable. When you reach this threshold, it will give you a competitive edge and serve as professional insurance. You will not need to compete with others. All you have to do is compete with yourself of the past and move ahead. With your added value to the office or workplace, you can make your boss's or team's work much easier. You may have noticed that there are experts in various sectors or industries who continue holding their influential positions even after major changes in leadership. They possess such valuable knowledge and skills that no leader can ignore them. They become irreplaceable. Their superior knowledge and expertise work as their job security.

You can aim to become an expert or a resource within your organization. You don't have to worry about your position. You can be an important person in any organization with or without a leadership position. Troubleshooters or experts always belong to the inner circle of any organization. They get special status within the team. Which boss doesn't want such a resource within their team to lighten their own workload? In fact, any reasonable boss will retain such a valuable person, rewarding their initiative. Increasing your value will mark a paradigm shift in your career. It will rescue you from obscurity and lead you to unlimited professional success.

Massive action is the single most powerful and determining factor of success. By taking massive action, you can build up, maintain and accelerate your success. This will take you from one success to another. For this, you must build a habit of going the extra mile. Remember: extraordinary success always lies far outside your comfort zone. To keep yourself competitive, you must keep practicing for longer hours in a similar way to a world-champion athlete. This will help you to step up to the next level. Start where you are right now; concentrate on one thing at a time. I can guarantee that by following this proven path, you will transform your life. When you go through this inner transformation, it will be reflected in every aspect of your life. You will be more self-confident than ever before.

Generally, average people give as little as possible in order to make maximum gains. To achieve success, you must move in the opposite direction. You must be willing to give more than you receive. You can invest your time, energy and money to achieve maximum impact in a single area. Most people chase after success without properly preparing themselves to reach their destination. Opportunities don't come along very often. Therefore, in order to catch an opportunity, you must keep yourself well prepared. Instead of chasing success, what you need to do is become more skillful and valuable. You can then utilize any opportunity. It's a development from within. When you reach this state, you will be self-assured. Sudden professional uncertainty will not unnerve you. You can continue your work without being frustrated. Irrespective of how others perceive you, you will remain confident. When you acquire new knowledge, skills and experience, you will attract success like a magnet. Useful skills are generally not taught in higher educational institutions. It's more a self-directed individual learning process. To achieve this, you must take the following steps.

GET THE FOCUS RIGHT

THE INVENTION OF SHOES

Long ago, when people lived without using shoes, a thought peeped into the mind of King Hobu. It interrupted his sleep that night. He said to Goburay, the chief minister, "You all draw a handsome salary every month, yet you cannot protect my royal feet from dust. If you cannot provide a solution to this problem soon, I will fire you." Hearing this, a bead of sweat ran down Goburay's forehead. He didn't want to lose his job. He lost sleep and his appetite trying to think of a solution. He met with intellectuals of the land appealing to them to help solve the problem. But no solution was found. Goburay said to the King, "If there is no dust on your feet, oh King, how will your subjects pay their respects?" Hobu said, "You are right, but you must first find a way to stop dust coming on my feet." Upon further advice from intellectuals, the chief minister came up with a solution. People with 1.7 million brooms were deployed to clean up all the dust. People of the land could not open their eyes due to dust floating on the air. Millions of people got sick as a result. Dust even struck the King's face and chest. The King was extremely annoyed. To solve the problem, 2.1

million buckets were deployed to pour water over the dusty land, using water from rivers, canals and ponds. Fishes and other water creatures died without water. Animals tried to swim in order to survive as the whole land was covered with clay. Intellectuals came up with another ingenious idea. They proposed to cover the land with carpets so that the King could avoid getting his feet dirty. Another suggestion was to isolate the King in his chambers so that he didn't see the dust. Hearing such outlandish and stupid propositions, a cobbler arrived at the Royal Palace. He said, "Your Highness, it's a simple problem with a simple solution. All you need to do is cover your feet with dried animal skin." He made shoes for the King and so the problem was resolved.

The above story is an adapted version of Rabindranath Tagore's popular Bengali poem *Juta abiskar* or *The Invention of Shoes*. The story clearly underlines the importance of focus in solving a problem or achieving success. The wrong focus can drain your time, energy and money. Even massive work may produce nothing useful or meaningful. The right focus, on the other hand, can achieve its goal with precision. There are many people in the world who live life aimlessly or with too broad a focus to fulfill their dreams. Even though they may possess superior knowledge and skills, this will not make them successful. Knowledge without a laser-like focus won't produce the expected results. Even actions may turn out to be futile. However, you may see people with little knowledge and resources become successful. It's due to their clarity of focus and concentration on one area. It is about acting with a clear focus. In other words, it is a directed action. This is a mindset that is much deeper than that led by impulse and appearance management. This requires that you focus on what is most important.

TAKE CONTROL OF YOUR TIME

Life in essence is the sum of time. As time is the most valuable resource in life, you must use it on the most important priorities. Seneca, a Roman Stoic philosopher, had argued that the right people don't have a short time in life. The problem is that many people fail to make the best use of it. All people of the world have same 24 hours in a day. Yet, using the same amount of time, some people become billionaires while many struggle to earn a living. To become successful, you have to be ruthlessly selective about how you spend your time. You should use it for maximizing professional output and adding value. Unfortunately, many people waste lots of their time in useless socializing, meetings and cheap entertainment. Seeing them, one may assume that they have plenty of time on their hands to spare. This is a suicidal tendency. If you do this, you should stop immediately. If you can't, you will regret it later. You must take full control of your time and use it with utmost care. You should objectively look at how you use your time daily. You must eliminate unproductive, unnecessary and useless time-consuming engagements. You need to be brutal about this. This will enable you to save time that you can invest in advancing your career.

For success, you must have weekly, monthly, yearly, five-yearly and even ten-yearly goals to achieve your targets. You have to use your time judiciously in order to increase your competitive edge in the marketplace. Most people get up at 6am or 7am and spend their weekdays in a workplace, as well as travelling to and from there. At work, they do regular and repetitive tasks as well as meetings, emailing and so on. When they return home, they look at social media newsfeeds on smartphones and watch TV. At 11pm or later, they go to bed. They waste lot of time during days and evenings, both online and in real life, in useless socialization without any clear goal or purpose. They just want to follow social trends. They gossip about celebrities in order to make sense of their otherwise empty lives. However, they fail to understand that it is impossible to increase one's value by following stories of famous people online or taking selfies with them and sharing those on social media. By blindly following others, they lose personal control over their time as well as happiness. Their happiness depends on the praise or approval of others. That's it. Nothing more. Spending time on celebrities won't produce anything useful unless you are a paparazzo or tabloid journalist. Instead, it will permanently disturb your peace of mind and create a sense of personal inadequacy. To get rid of this shallow living, you must focus on yourself. You must make a personalized career plan and spend time carrying out purposeful activities.

You must free up time from your daily routine in order to work on yourself. How can you create some extra hours every day and use it for professional development? To do this, you should go to bed earlier in the evening and get up earlier in the morning. You should understand that it will be beneficial for your health, wealth and wisdom, as it is suggested in the well-known rhyme. When you get up early, you can use this time for increasing professional knowledge and skills. If possible, you should consider making it a habit to get out of bed as early as 4:30 am. I personally do this. It has, in fact, transformed my career and life. Initially it may appear a daunting task. However, after the initial weeks, the most challenging time, it will become easier to follow. Later on, it will seem automatic and part of your personality. When you do this, you can add at least extra three hours of practice before going to your regular day-time job. You can use this time for increasing professional knowledge and honing new skills. As a good reader myself, I suggest you read books or practice your professional craft in the early hours. This will give you the edge over others. During your journey to and from work, you can read a book or a journal. Some busy and successful people even use their daily travelling hours to do their professional writing. When you consistently use extra hours for reading or mastering your craft for a longer period, you will surely get ahead of others in your career. You will be more valued in your professional field. Your level of self-confidence will increase significantly.

If you are a student, hours of extra studies will keep you ahead of your fellow students. If you are an unemployed person, you can spend five to eight hours every day on developing your knowledge and skills. In this digital age, you can use the power of social media to accelerate your career progression. In addition to reading books, professional journals and practicing your craft, you can also watch YouTube videos or listen to podcasts to update your professional knowledge by following the leading figures of your industry. To keep track of your time, you can create a routine and follow it. It is also important to keep a large year planner hanging on your wall. This will give you a clear sense of control over your time.

Through regular daily reading or practice of your craft for a longer period, you can increase your professional knowledge and skills. It will help you to stand out and get an edge over others in any competitive situation. If you are an unemployed, you can also work as a volunteer in an organization. It will help you get much-needed work experience. This will enable you to break the vicious cycle of unemployment. What separates world champions from other athletes is their solo practice. They practice for longer hours than others. People get surprised by seeing players win Olympic golds. But they don't see a sportsperson's practice for hours and hours every day to build up their competitive edge.

Paavo Nurmi, the legendary Finnish middle- and long-distance runner won nine Olympic gold medals, and a total of twelve Olympic medals at three Olympic Games from 1920 to 1928. He was known as *"The Flying Finn"*. As a mark of honor, a portrait of Nurmi was issued on the erstwhile ten-mark bank note prior to introduction of the Euro in Finland. His success was attributed to his training and fanatical practice.

I earned my PhD from the University of Helsinki in 2004 and soon afterwards joined as a postdoctoral researcher with a research team at the University of Tampere. As my fixed-term job contract ended in 2007, I became unemployed. I lived in Helsinki for a year and applied for various jobs. But I failed to get one. Then I left

Finland for the United Kingdom in search of a job. I lived in London for a year. After that, I moved to Bangladesh and spent three years attempting to make a career breakthrough. Still I was unable to create career success in my native land. By leaving my wife and children behind, I went to Toronto, Canada, stayed in a friend's home and applied for jobs. After that, I returned to Finland. That time, I was literally broke. In addition, I had many hundred thousand takas of loans in Bangladesh and a big student loan to pay back in Finland. I could not take this humiliating circumstance any more.

One day, I took a very important decision that instead of looking for a job only, I would focus on my personal development. In order to increase my expertise, I would read books and other published materials of my niche for at least six hours every day no matter what. I carried out my plan accordingly. In the meantime, my family members were reunited with me in Finland. Finnish summer is an enjoyable time after a long, snowy, cold and dark season. Schools remain closed during most of the summer time. Even during the beautiful Finnish summer days, as well as the nights of 2014–2016, I sat in my study reading books for hours. Sometimes, my wife and kids got bored with me, as I could not accompany them outside to parks or the Baltic Sea shores. I explained my plan to them. They understood and supported me.

My hard work paid off. In addition to my background as a researcher in Finland, I established myself as a highly-valued expert in my field. Since then, whichever job I joined, I was highly appreciated. All organizations gave me greater responsibilities and showered me with praise. I worked for the Peace Union of Finland.

Later, I was elected as a board member of two nongovernmental organizations, PEN Finland and the Humanist Association of Finland. Both organizations provided me with the opportunity to develop myself further. In PEN Finland, I worked to protect the rights of writers and journalists worldwide. Initially, I served as the chair of its Writers for Peace Committee and later as the chair of the Writers at Risk Committee. I participated in the Writers at Risk Committee meeting of PEN International in Lillehammer, Norway, in 2017. As a PEN Finland delegate, I also represented it in the PEN International Annual Congress in Ukraine and India, in 2017 and 2018 respectively. I drafted a good number of statements and resolutions that were approved by PEN International. Many of those were circulated to over a hundred PEN centers worldwide. In 2018, PEN International invited me to work as a researcher at its headquarters in London. I was excited to use my new level of expertise and learn from my colleagues there. It was a breathtaking experience. I also visited officials of English PEN in London and Scottish PEN in Edinburgh, as well as meeting several MPs in the House of Commons and the Scottish Parliament.

Those were my voluntary self-directed roles that I enjoyed, by synchronizing them with the PEN team. I knew my subject extremely well and worked passionately from my heart. However, in order to concentrate on writing my book, I resigned from Finnish PEN in May 2019. Influential leaders of PEN Finland and PEN International were shocked by my decision. Several said that the whole PEN community lost an "asset". Hearing the news of my resignation from PEN Finland, a core expert of the PEN

International team in London wrote to me, "What a loss for them and for us!" I miss a good number of extraordinary people I had the opportunity to meet in both PEN Finland and PEN International. But life must move forward. It was so hard for me to give up these voluntary responsibilities that I truly loved. However, now I am ready to take up another larger mission. I want to inspire others to success by using my earned knowledge, wisdom and skills. This book is the manifestation of this aspiration. I was born in an average family in a Bangladeshi village. If I can achieve this success, you too can achieve any success!

START FROM WHERE YOU ARE NOW

Many people think that to start the success process, you must go somewhere else or reach a certain level and then start from there. This is a wrong approach for which you may pay a price. You may reach your goals too late or may never reach them at all. By thinking in this way, you may end up with only procrastination, failure and misery. Rather, you should start your pursuit of success right from where you are at this moment. Success is, in fact, all about building inner resourcefulness. You can strengthen or amplify your inner resources by staying in your natural environment and working on yourself. Unplanned ambitious goals will not help you. In fact, they may derail you from success. They can ruin your finances and life. If you have the right vision and purpose, your place of residence should not be a barrier to achieving success. There is a proverb that where there is a will, there is a way. Instead of pursing money, first and foremost you should develop your personal resourcefulness. It is the magic key of success.

You must plan carefully and use every opportunity to develop yourself locally. I must admit that, I made mistakes in my career path. At the end of my job contract with Tampere University, Finland, as a senior researcher in 2007, I spent one year applying for jobs in Finland. After that, instead improving my professional skills, I went abroad to find a regular job. I sent my family members to Bangladesh and moved to the United Kingdom as a jobseeker. I spent four years in the United Kingdom, Bangladesh and Canada in pursuit of meaningful work without success. After this period, I returned to Finland heavily in debt. I was one the verge of bankruptcy. It took years for me to recover to a normal financial condition again. Overall, I must admit that it was a costly venture for me and my family. However, it also worked as a valuable lesson for me. I got personal insights about the real world and how it works.

There are no hard and fast rules or conditions for you to start your quest for success. If you have the right vision, you can start the process from where you are now. By using inner resourcefulness, you can create success from anywhere. The location does not matter. The grass always appears greener elsewhere. But, first of all, you have to look at your own ground and make the best use of your environment to create results. If you currently have a day job and intend to pursue a new career, it is sensible that you don't quit your current work. Rather, you should keep your job and make a career transition by doing this side by side in your spare time. This way you can save yourself from sudden financial risks.

Remember that if you are a non-professional in your own country, you will also be considered the same in other countries as well. The same applies if you are a professional or skilled person. If you are a professional in Africa, Asia, Latin America or anywhere else, you remain a professional – irrespective of your income level in your home country. If you relocate to Europe, North America or elsewhere as an immigrant, you should keep your professional identity intact. If possible, don't give it up. It is more important to keep your professional identity in a developed country than surrendering your profession for immediate financial gain. Your professional identity should define you, not your country of residence or citizenship. I therefore strongly recommend you to build up a professional identity. In whatever circumstances you are in, never lose your hope and dignity. Respect yourself as a person and handle the situation with courage. Irrespective of your country or place of residence, make yourself skillful by using local resources. If the educational and professional qualifications system is very different in the new country, you may have to pursue some additional studies, skills or work experience to keep yourself as a professional. If you do this, you won't regret it later.

GO BEYOND YOUR COMFORT ZONE

Success always lies outside one's comfort zone. Many people can have ambitious goals of achieving success in life. However, all are not ready to go beyond their comfort zones. Only a selected minority can make it. The majority of people drop out before reaching their goals due to the fact that they find the process difficult. Success is found when preparation meets opportunity.

Every overweight person dreams of living life with a normal weight. Some may go to the gym to lose weight and others may opt for a diet. However, the majority of them lose interest within the first two to three weeks because they cannot stand being outside their comfort zone. In other words, they don't have compelling enough reasons to continue with the difficult process. It also reflects their lack of individual commitment to achieve their goal. When you know that failure is not an option and you are ready to go through whatever it takes to achieve success, then you will definitely be successful.

In order to achieve your goals, you have to give up over-analyzing things. Even people with superior knowledge and skills cannot act and achieve desired results if they are over-cautious. It's harmful. You must go beyond your comfort zone in order to increase your value in the marketplace and attract success. It's impossible to achieve valuable skills and experience without going outside your comfort zone. If it was not so, everybody could be successful. Success would not have any special meaning then. You have to push yourself harder to test how much discomfort you can endure. By stretching yourself to this zone, you can acquire new skills and experiences. Everything worthwhile in life has a price tag attached to it. You never get something for nothing. Things you get too easily, or for free, generally have less value and significance. Of course, the human body and health are notable exceptions to this. If you want to acquire something worthwhile in life, you must embrace uncertainty and keep pushing beyond the limit of your ability. With determined action and discipline, you can make things possible.

I came across many South Asian immigrants in Finland, Europe and North America. A large proportion of them opted for initiating small enterprises, such as opening pizza shops and restaurants in their adopted countries, and gained economic solvency. After moving to these countries as students or political asylum-seekers, they built up a better life for themselves and their families by defying linguistic and other barriers. Initially, the majority of them lacked sufficient capital to open up a new small business. Yet they overcame those hurdles with sheer resolve, building capital through doing jobs and taking loans from friends. There are instances where within five years, they not only made their enterprise profitable, but some of them were also able to open a second or third business as well. Instead of becoming a burden to society, they created job opportunities not only for themselves but also for the locals. Going beyond their comfort zone created this miracle called "immigrant success stories". It is a surprising fact that many of those restaurant owners never had any experience cooking in their country of birth.

Educational reformer John Dewey underlined the importance of taking deliberate efforts and thoughtful pains in achieving success. It is important that your actions should speak louder than your words. To avoid regret, you must go beyond your comfort zone and test your limits. When you endure hardships and discomforts for a higher goal, then you unlock the doors to success. The top successful people of the world got out of their comfort zones by challenging themselves. When you can challenge yourself to achieve your goal, you get access to the master key of your success. When you reach this stage, literally, you can achieve anything in life. Note that success doesn't depend on luck or circumstances. It requires meticulous planning and repeated action with such zeal as if it were the only option left for you. It is as if your life depended on it. It's a matter of spirit. It's about setting a worthy goal and achieving it by overcoming yourself. Lots of mental and physical work are involved here. It's about overcoming yourself.

CONCENTRATE ON ONE THING AT A TIME

In many countries, the government machinery is run by generalists. Government officials are equipped with general knowledge of state, market and society. However, there is less space provided for specialists with specific technical skills. As a result, the full capacity of administration remains underutilized. To address this issue, countries need more people with specialized knowledge and skills. Similarly, on an individual level too, it is important to find your niche to narrow down your areas of competence in a focused way. By conducting focused actions, it is possible to perform better and achieve more personal effectiveness. You should concentrate your strengths on one thing with a laser-like focus to achieve concrete results. It is a powerful tool for achieving effectiveness in work. If you put a piece of paper close under a magnifying glass, under a scorching sun, the concentrated energy of the rays will burn the paper within minutes. This is an example of the power of concentration.

The Japanese *Kaizen* principle shows us the power of small steps to accomplish larger goals in the long run. It's about taking small steps every day to improve a habit or process, keeping in mind the long-term goal. It is a powerful tool for improving oneself and developing a product or a service. Japanese car maker Toyota has been using this principle as its core value, ensuring the quality and reliability of its cars. You can also use it to improve your skills. As it does not produce an immediate result, one may fail to see its power. But it is a slow and steady process that can bring excellence in your professional life. Rightly followed, it can work as a silent revolution for you. Small steps can improve a habit, a process or product. By following this principle, you can ensure continuous improvement, maintain excellence and realize personal dreams. Human brains are naturally resistant to change. However, small steps can help you to reduce anxiety, fear and resistance. Over a longer period, this can help you in achieving larger success.

TAKE MASSIVE ACTION

To achieve massive success, you must take massive action. There is no alternative to this. It's a matter of being deeply committed to achieving your goals. This is different from routine superficial actions which are taken without a true inner urge. When you can dedicate your time, energy and money to achieve your goals, you become massively successful. Dedicated actions not only produce results but also help you to attain higher levels of confidence. This requires a burning desire or a deep passion. It's different from acting mechanically to comply with outside pressure or being attracted to a goal without a deeply-felt sense of purpose. When your desire for success comes from the heart and is connected to a higher purpose in life, it will pull you towards success with a strong natural force. No hurdle will be able to stop you from reaching your goal. It will motivate you to take actions for career goals. You will complete a task within a timeframe no matter what. While talent or innate capability has a role in career success, massive practice over an extended period of time is a determining factor in achieving extraordinary results. Preparation and completion of tasks are keys to success. There are no shortcuts.

When you take repeated actions with consistency and discipline over an extended period of time, your performance becomes automatic. Through this, you can transform your life – similar to the metamorphosis that occurs when a caterpillar turns into a butterfly. The hard work is worth the rewards. You must stay committed when you follow this process. It makes you feel good about yourself. If you want to be a world-class expert or performer in any field, you must take dedicated action on a daily, weekly, monthly and yearly basis. You must be consistent no matter what. Through repetition, you can build up new habits and take your skills to a higher level. By doing so for a long time, your actions will become effortless and automatic. Researchers who study expertise have found that you need 10,000 hours of practice for attaining mastery in any field. To achieve this, one needs to work with clear focus, concentration, discipline and persistence.

To increase your value in the marketplace, you must do your best and be your best. You must act with a blueprint. You must continue your actions with consistency, no matter what. This will pave the way for making yourself the master of your own life. This is the most wonderful thing that can happen to a person. When you reach this state, it will be reflected in all aspects of your life. In this state, you look at your inner substance, rather than looking outwards. When you achieve this state, you will not need to engage in petty workplace politics. Rather, your quality will speak for itself and will determine your place in your industry. It can be a truly liberating experience. In this state, instead of anger towards your jealous critics and haters, you will feel sorry for them. A combination of hard work and self-discipline will protect your interests. If you need help charting this unique path, it is worthwhile getting a mentor. Initially, this book will serve as a mentor for you.

People often attempt to mystify success. You should not lend your ears to any such myth. Nothing but consistent practice is the key to all small and big successes in life. If a person self-educates and reaches a higher threshold of knowledge and skills in a specialized field, he may not need to get a high school, college or university diploma. A diploma may be irrelevant to his real needs.

Nobel literature laureate Rabindranath Tagore is still one of the towering figures in South Asian and world literature almost eight decades after his death. He was a great poet, songwriter, novelist, playwright and philosopher. He was an avid reader. However, he did not possess a high school diploma. He was home-educated or self-educated. Does it mean that if you want to be massively successful, you don't need to pursue formal education, or you need to dropout from your studies? Not exactly. Tagore took such massive actions in pursuit of his passion that it was not necessary for him to get any diploma. A diploma was irrelevant to his career needs. Instead, he used his time for reading and creative writing. By doing so, he established himself as a towering intellectual figure of the world. He was against parochial nationalism. He advocated greater East-West collaboration for the progress of humanity. With his remarkable humanistic ideas, he challenged the traditional schooling system. He founded a unique school at Shantiniketan for fulfilling learners' individual needs, self-reliance, practical skills, freedom of mind and creating a harmonious relationship with the world. Later in 1951, it became Visva-Bharati University.

By taking massive action, you will be able to move from one success to another. You will enjoy taking on new challenges. In this animated state, you can break your own previous success record to make new records. You will attain the mindset of a champion. With this mindset, you will be able to create a better version of yourself each and every day. You will become unstoppable.

DEVELOP NEW HABITS FOR ACQUIRING SKILLS

For real success in life, you must acquire knowledge and skills. There are scores of books and journals for your industry or specialization written by well-known experts of your field. You can seek out and start reading these on a regular basis. Reading will end your guesswork and ignorance on any subject matter and make you a well-informed person. This is like a nutrient for your mind. By reading, you will build up neurons in your brain. Literally, it is the muscle power of your brain. By putting special emphasis on acquiring knowledge and skills, you can advance yourself professionally. To do this, you will need to read books and journals, as well as attending seminars and conferences, joining courses and using social media. By equipping yourself with better knowledge and insight, you can serve the needs of others or solve their problems. By making yourself useful to others, you can enjoy the journey itself. It's the journey of becoming. It's not a mere search for material gains. It's about increasing your skills, competence and value in the marketplace.

When you can shift your focus from material gain to becoming a valuable person by working on yourself, it will have a profound impact on your career success. It will change your life. From my personal experience, I can guarantee that if you follow this mantra in your life, you will never look back again. You will become a highly-successful person. For success, you don't need to get involved in narrow office politics and undermine others in order to show yourself in a positive light to your superiors. Just work on yourself in order to increase your skills and experience. Don't blame others for your condition. Rather, increase your value in the marketplace.

To use your time effectively, you must follow your daily routine no matter what. You must focus on important tasks over urgent ones. Humans are slaves of their habits. Social and cultural conditioning are responsible for much of people's everyday behavior. They do things automatically without realizing that they are following a process. For achieving career success, you must develop new success habits. Those who have researched the subject suggest that one needs around three weeks of practice at the least to develop a new habit. By establishing clear focus and maintaining repetition every day on a consistent basis, you can develop a new habit. By practicing for longer hours and a longer period, you can consolidate and make it part of your nature or personality. When you reach this state, it may seem effortless.

Repetition is the key to forming a habit. However, long-term vision, internal drive and strong concentration play significant roles in this process. If you can connect development of a new habit with a new improved version of yourself, it can work as a strong motivator for you. In other words, the spirit makes the difference. There is a difference between a person who wants to acquire a habit in order to impress others and a self-driven person who associates the new habit with relief from pain and attainment of pleasure. While the first person will be less motivated to do the work, the second person will be highly motivated to act, defying all odds.

To achieve success, you must make an investment in high-return skills development. Reading is such an important life-changing undertaking. Through this, you can add exceptional value in your professional life. It sharpens your mind. It hugely contributes to personal growth. Finland is a role model for the rest of the world in terms of high standards of living, human development and many other sectors. If you want to understand the most important characteristic of Finnish people that separates them from other nations, it is people's reading habits. Finnish people are great readers. If you visit Finland, you will see the common sight of people reading in buses, trains, metros, trams and parks. Public libraries are part and parcel of people's lives. In some countries of the world, the elite collect books for their shelves for the purpose of impressing others with their good taste and cultural sophistication. In fact, many don't read their books at all. They are so preoccupied with other things that they don't have time for reading. But in Finland, you will be surprised by the personal collection of books of the average Finnish person. And they do read their collection of books. It makes them well-informed citizens of Finland, as well as the globe.

Reading books is extremely important for your personal growth and success. A single idea can change your life for the better. It can open doors for extraordinary career success. By absorbing the ideas of great books, you can transform yourself into a more valuable person. Because of this, it is important to read important books that may boost your career. You may attend courses, seminars and conferences to update your professional knowledge and skills. If you intend to take your career to a new height, you must invest in your personal development. It will increase your market value as well taking your self-confidence to the next level. The more you invest in personal development, the faster you will achieve a higher level of professional competence. Let's say that you if buy fifty books in a year for reading, in five years you will possess two hundred and fifty books. By reading two hundred and fifty books, you can significantly increase your professional knowledge, skills and competence. If the price of one book on average is 20 Euros, in five years you will spend 5,000 Euros. This means, in a month you will buy around four books. It will cost you around 80 Euros only. Is this a big amount of money? Of course not. How much money do you spend every month on coffees, cigarettes, buying things and eating out? Comparing to such big spending, it's a very small expense. If you can cut unproductive and unnecessary expenditure, you can even spend 200–500 Euros per month on buying books and investing in other forms of personal development. Imagine how much benefit you may reap in the long run by spending this money. When you add extraordinary value in your career, you will attract success like a magnet. People of your profession that matter to you will not be able to ignore you. This will work as a guarantee for your job security. Your race, color, religion, gender, height, weight or appearance etc. will not matter. If you become an entrepreneur, you can make profits and become a billionaire.

With the aid of a powerful search engine such as Google and a video-sharing website such as YouTube, you have information at your fingertips. You just need a smart phone or a PC with Internet connection. You can improve any area of your life by getting useful information, watching and listening to valuable videos and practicing the skill you want to acquire daily. You can read books borrowed from public libraries. It's the most cost-effective way of reading books. However, you may find that some books are not available in libraries. Also, you may not be able to borrow a book of your choice since it may be borrowed by another reader. At times, waiting for the book can be frustrating. I personally prefer to buy valuable books from prominent bookstores. I also buy books during my foreign trips. During my time living in London from 2007–2008, I was a regular reader at the British Library as well as Whitechapel's Idea Store and many libraries in East London. I also bought many books and watched many world-famous movies. My favorite bookshop in London is Waterstones in Trafalgar Square. Whenever I visit the city nowadays, I take the opportunity to buy books from here. There is an advantage to buying books over borrowing from libraries: you can underline text and make notes on pages as you wish. This enables you to easily find information later when you need to. It saves your time and makes you an effective writer.

In Finland, I used to regularly buy and order books from abroad through the main Akateeminen kirjakauppa (Academic Bookstore) in Helsinki city center during 2014-16. During this period, hardly a week passed when I did not buy books and order books from abroad. Sometimes I ordered even seven books at a time. Over the past three years alone, I bought over three hundred books. Those books are from various branches of knowledge including philosophy, history, psychology, education, religion and many other topics. I became a recognizable face to the staff at the store. One day, a member of staff delivered half a dozen books that had arrived for me from abroad. Smiling, she said, "May I ask you a question? Do you read all those books you order, or do you collect those for other people?" I loved the question. Smiling back at her, I replied, "Yes, of course I buy books for myself. But I haven't managed time to read them all yet." I took the questions as recognition of me being an avid reader.

Besides reading, you may accelerate your success through serving as a volunteer. Competition for jobs is high, both in public and private sectors. People are programmed in such a way that they want to get regular paid jobs. As a result, there is huge competition for advertised positions. In certain countries of high-density population, competition is too high. Sometimes, it can be beyond belief – there can be up to five hundred candidates or more for a single position. A job is like a golden deer. Everybody wants to catch it at any cost. Unemployed youths face a chicken-egg dilemma while attempting to get a job. Without experience, they cannot get a job. Without work, how can they get experience? To make a breakthrough in this situation you can offer to volunteer in an organization that works in your field of interest.

If you are a fresh graduate and want to break into the job market, this will provide you with useful experience. If you are unemployed, volunteering will help to break the cycle of unemployment. Overall, volunteerism offers you with the opportunity to develop yourself professionally and build up personal rapport with a manager. If you work with dedication and professionalism, you will get a good reference from the office. This will help you to get a regular job in the future. If you can contribute to the organization in a useful and valuable way as a volunteer, when a regular position opens up, your boss may consider you for that position. In almost all sectors, it's your proven track record that plays a decisive role in the final recruitment decision. While building up a good CV and sending applications to potential employers are important for making you visible among applicants in a recruitment process, proven skills and track record are more important than you may think. Bosses feel comfortable with people they have had a previous good experience with. In order to make a career breakthrough, you should offer yourself as a volunteer. Another way of increasing your career skills and advancing your career is to offer yourself as a volunteer teacher in the community. This will help you with retaining your newly-earned knowledge in your field, as well as contributing to community development. The by-product of voluntary teaching is that you will be confident in communicating your message to the audience. In the long run, it will open up new avenues for your career and life success.

GET MENTORS

Mentors play an important role in career success. Parents, teachers and managers serve as mentors to other people. Contemporary, as well as past, thinkers and writers can also serve as mentors to people through their books. I was born in a Bangladeshi village. I spent a part of my childhood in a joint family headed by my grandfather. Later, I spent most of my childhood and youth in small towns across Bangladesh with my parents. I lived in Dhaka for ten years while I pursued my studies at college and university. Later, I spent two and half decades in Finland and Europe. From childhood, my parents supported me to the best of their abilities. Teachers from my primary schools, high schools, college and university advised me and helped me in shaping the course of my life. They are the true heroes of my life. There are also other people who contributed to advancing my life and career. Abdus Sobhan, a primary school teacher of mine at Barhatta town and Dr. Nazmul Ahsan Kalimullah, a professor of Dhaka University, were big influences on me through their assistance and unconventional ideas. Currently, Kalimullah is serving as the Vice-Chancellor of Begum Rokeya University, Rangpur. Sobhan showed me the way to build a life of inner richness by defying social conformity. Kalimullah showed me the way to connect to the world through volunteerism.

I came to Finland as an international student to pursue my higher education back in 1996. I obtained my PhD from the University of Helsinki in 2004, writing and publishing a dissertation on international education. Moving from a lecture-oriented to a research-oriented educational environment was a big challenge for me. My PhD research supervisor professor Dr. Ilkka Heiskanen, and later professor Dr. Risto Eräsaari, both internationally-reputed Finnish academics, patiently helped me to polish my research skills. It is fair to say that they transformed my life and helped me find a far better direction.

I also came across academics and writers as well as democracy, peace and human rights leaders and activists. In some, I saw a higher level of professional standards, humility, selflessness and idealism. Sirpa Kähkönen is one of these people. Kähkönen is an award-winning Finnish writer who is popular for her Kuopio series of historical novels. She holds an Honorary Doctorate degree of Åbo Academy University of Finland. She was the former president of PEN Finland and the current president of the Finnish Writers' Union. Seeing my level of professional knowledge and expertise while in PEN, she facilitated and paved the way for me, as a board member and the chair of the Writers at Risk Committee, to represent the organization in various meetings of PEN International. Though I previously did fieldwork in Asia and Africa and presented research papers in various conferences in European countries as a researcher, representing PEN Finland in PEN International meetings and annual Congresses boosted my professional skills and self-confidence to a new level. Before PEN, I possessed a PhD and had academic knowledge, however, my communication skills were poor. This had held me back from fulfilling my true potential. But not any more. After my active and successful roles in PEN for over three years, I'm now a transformed person with a new mission.

Whatever level of the professional and life ladder you are on, this book will help you to plan and pursue your career. It will work as your mentor or guide. To increase your professional skills, you may consider enrolling yourself in course or a program. Nowadays, you don't necessarily need to go to a university to obtain useful skills. There are many affordable offline and online courses in which you can enroll to sharpen your competence. These will enable you to remain relevant in the job market. We are living in an age of digital revolution that is disrupting many traditional professions. The dominant pattern of a job as a lifelong and permanent vocation is changing. In the future, millions of jobs in well-established professions will simply disappear due to the introduction of automation and artificial intelligence. This will also create millions of new jobs that require technical skills. In the future, jobs will be strongly skills-based and part-time in nature. There will be lots of flexibility in work. You will be able to do your job remotely by staying at home. In these changing times, cutting-edge and marketable skills will help you to keep yourself relevant in the marketplace. Adding additional skills to your portfolio will enable you to tackle future challenges effectively.

Considering the changing nature of work and your need to stay relevant in the marketplace, you should get mentors. A mentor is an accomplished professional who can help you to uncover your strengths, weaknesses and potential. You can learn and practice the successful techniques used by him or her to create your own success. As higher-level professionals of any field are extremely busy, you may consider reaching out to a career coach who can help you. It may cost you money, but getting a coach will help you to accelerate your career success much faster. A coach will show you the way. But you have to do the rest. You have to increase your skills to make yourself valuable in the marketplace. This is a self-driven process. No one will see the hard work you do behind the scenes. However, if you get this right, you will achieve amazing returns. People will be amazed at your success. They will think that it is matter of luck. But you will know what it is exactly. Once you reach this state, you achieve one success after another. You will get promoted in your profession time and again. If you are in business, you will earn a fortune. You will also feel the positive impact on your personal and social life. As a byproduct of this, you will become well known, perhaps even famous.

SELF-ASSESSMENT/ACTIONS

List three areas of high-return investment in your personal development.

1. ____

2. ____

3. ____

List three key actions you must take to make a career breakthrough.

1. ____

2. ____

3. ____

List timeframes for achieving your three key goals.

1. ____

2. ____

3. ____

List the three most important actions/habits you want to build that will give you maximum returns.

1. ____

2. ____

3. ____

List your time allocation in hours for developing a new habit (daily, weekly and monthly).

1. ____

2. ____

3. ____

List three benchmarks to measure your progress in achieving your goals.

1. ____

2. ____

3. ____

CHAPTER 8

RECREATE YOURSELF

To create a new version of yourself, you will need to acquire new knowledge, skills and experiences. Your positive attitude, clarity of purpose, skills and authenticity will refine you as a person. This will open up new windows of opportunity for you professionally as well as personally. It's an individual journey of becoming more resourceful and more valuable in the marketplace. In this journey, there is no limit to your success. You can be as successful as you want to be. All you need is to take a conscious decision to embrace this path. When you embark on this journey and carry out tasks, you will be successful. Initial success will motivate you to achieve more and more successes. So, celebrate small successes. You must keep in mind that the journey will not be easy. But as long as you have a vision and roadmap, temporary setbacks will not deter you from your course of action. You will enjoy the journey itself and develop resilience for facing challenges. As you take ownership of your plan and action, you will remain in the driving seat of your life.

Working on your personal development will make you a confident person. You will feel good about yourself. Your inner self-confidence and willpower will be reflected in your outer behavior and performance.

Simply by adopting a positive attitude and focusing on the bigger picture, you will see life from a new perspective. Instead of weaknesses, limitations, pains, fears and failures, you will see life as full of possibility. You will discover that your life has magically moved from negative to positive territory. Your thinking will shift from "I cannot" to "Yes, I can." You will feel highly energetic and driven. Initially, changes may seem uncomfortable and even scary to a certain extent. Critics and even friends may laugh at you, seeing the changes. However, if you go with clear objectives, concrete actions and discipline, I can assure you that these will reward you handsomely in the long run. You will not only survive the criticism of naysayers, but also reach new heights of career success.

As discussed earlier, the longer hours you practice every day for a longer period, the faster you can acquire a new habit. If you can practice at least three to four hours every day for a period of three months, it can give you a strong footing to form a new habit and reach your milestone. The more you practice, the better you get in your craft. Your initial success will motivate you to take further action. By continuing the same practice, you can earn industry-level skills and expertise within two to three years. In five to ten years, you can become a nationally- and even an internationally-recognized expert in your field. When you pursue this path, you will be surprised at your own level of success. In the long run, everything will seem effortless and natural. The bottom line is, you must broaden your knowledge and skills all the time to keep yourself up to date and competitive in the marketplace. When the right opportunity arises, you must seize it.

For extraordinary success, you must become an extraordinary person with high-industry level knowledge, expertise and skills. You must improve interpersonal communication too. When you master communication skills, you will be able to clearly articulate and express your thoughts. You will become an attractive person. When you reach this stage, you will start liking yourself more than ever before. You will feel like a celebrity or star. You will bear and carry the standard of excellence. The things you touch will turn to gold. You will become an asset to any organization or industry. You will also inspire others to success. This personal transformation is life-changing. To reach this level, you don't necessarily need to hold a formal leadership position. Modern leadership is less about a position and more about building up yourself as a skilled, valuable, effective and likable professional. You can achieve these qualities without a formal position. When you become such a valuable asset to your office or industry, I guarantee that you will be showered with rewards. Through your valuable contribution, you will become a leader with or without a formal position. Your important contributions to the organization will make you a core group member. You will be essential and irreplaceable. Essentially, you will become a king – even without an official crown. As you add tremendous value to the organization, you will be rewarded with promotions and other benefits. You will be offered leadership positions. You will be the envy of many of your colleagues. If you are an entrepreneur, you can become a billionaire.

Imagine your friends had known you as a shy and tongue-tied individual whose sole aim of life was to get a regular paid job. Now, after twelve years, you have transformed yourself by attaining a high level of professional knowledge, communication skills and leadership qualities. You are in a leadership position. Now you are ready to step up to the next level. Will it not be fascinating for you to show this improved version of yourself to your friends? Will they not join you in celebrating your success? Naturally, they will. It is said that success has many fathers, but failure is an orphan. When you are successful, even strangers will be friendly towards you. But during hard times or when one loses a fortune, even your nearest and dearest can simply disappear from the scene leaving you alone.

Uncontrolled materialism can spoil the soul of people. In this situation, if you still have one or two caring family members or friends by your side, you are extremely lucky. Legendary Indian film director Vasant Kumar Shivashankar Padukone, popularly known as Guru Dutt, and Orson Welles's famous movies portrayed the wanton materialism of an acquisitive society that stamps on sensitive human souls. One of the core messages of such movies is that though money may be an important tool for fulfilling many basic needs, it cannot buy you happiness. Bear in mind that disappointments and disillusionment are a natural part of human life. You need to build your own personal capacity to withstand harsh realities no matter what ladder of success you are standing on. You must save yourself first in order to save the world.

Revolution after revolution throughout human history have had their intrigues, conspiracies and failures. Even powerful people had been betrayed by apparently loyal friends in their inner circle. It was usually a question of personal or group interest that initiated the back-stabbings or assassinations. However, unlike other revolutions, personal development will never betray you. The conscious revolution of personal development will help you to create an "inner" safe haven to face the unexpected. Whenever needed, you can take refuge there. Even if the whole world turns against you, you will not lose faith in yourself. You can fully depend on yourself no matter what. Greek philosopher and one of the founders of Western philosophy, Socrates, had such a rich inner world. Accused being a corrupter of youth, he faced an unfair trial. However, he didn't retreat from his principles. After the verdict, he gladly drank poison *hemlock* and embraced death. He died without regrets.

If you follow the guidelines of this book, you will earn fortune, personal power and inner resilience. You will be in a position to positively influence and serve hundreds, thousands or even millions of people. You will be able to build a "dream life" worth living. By cultivating the following habits and qualities in your life, together with attaining professional knowledge and skills, you will earn massive career success. You will achieve a life of your dreams. Your life will be a true adventure. You will enjoy the journey itself. You will be a unique and remarkable person in your own right.

DO PHYSICAL EXERCIZES

We are living in a world of abundance. This is far better time than any other in human history. In addition to the highly-industrialized nations such as the USA, Canada, Europe, Australia,

Japan as well as East and Southeast Asian nations, more and more countries are catching up economically. The rise of China, India, Brazil, South Africa and many other Asian, African and Latin American countries is bringing a more comfortable life for citizens. The middle class is rising in many parts of the world. Nowadays, less people die of hunger around the world. Better nutrition and access to healthcare contribute to increased life expectancy. More and more people die from diseases of affluence such as type two diabetes, hypertension, cardiovascular diseases, cancer, etc. Most of such diseases emanate from over-eating and lack of manual labor or physical exercise. It is no wonder that when people do less manual work, they spend more of their time watching TV and checking social media news feeds on their smartphones. Researchers suggest that physical exercise also thwarts dementia in older people and stimulates the brain. So, to keep yourself fit for success, do regular physical exercises as a matter of priority. It will help you to live a healthy and effective life. Do physical exercise or walk for at least an hour every day as part of your daily routine. Make it a part of your career and life success plan.

BE TRUSTWORTHY

For massive success, you must become a reliable and trustworthy person. In this world there are some people who are clever, smart, outgoing and apparently successful. Yet others don't trust them because of their opportunist or manipulative behavior. They may attempt to create a good first impression to others through exaggeration of their abilities and a pretense of empathy for others. However, as time passes by, their true character is revealed through their actions. If you cannot keep consistency between your words and actions, you will lose your credibility with others. Without trust there can be no meaningful relationship. Nobody wants to do business with a known liar or a manipulative person. Everybody wants to avoid such untrustworthy people. To become truly successful, you must cultivate a good heart and become a good human being. Otherwise, material success will not bring you inner happiness or fulfilment.

To build up trust, you have to go the extra mile and do the extra work. You must bring harmony between talk and action. You must walk your talk. You must work on improving yourself. You have to contribute to others without expecting immediate rewards. You must keep in mind that creating trust is an investment. Your credibility is an extremely important asset that you must protect with utmost zeal; it's about protecting your personal brand. While you may pursue a path of learning and success, this means nothing if it is not backed up with authenticity. Whatever you do, do it passionately and wholeheartedly. Over time, people understand the difference between a reliable and an unreliable person. You cannot fool all the people all the time. For success, shun superficiality and embrace authenticity.

BE AN ACTIVE LISTENER

Many people consider communication as a tool for merely expressing yourself, but it is a two-way process. Because of this, you must first listen to others and then express yourself. To recreate yourself as a balanced person, you must control your ego and develop a habit of listening to others. It will help in making your communication mutual and effective. Generally, when one person meets another, they each carry their own messages in their minds. Unintentionally, it becomes more of a predetermined or scripted talk that provides little or no room for responding to the other person's mood, interests or needs. This type of communication may turn out to be a one-sided, boring monologue or lecture. For the other side, it is not an interesting encounter. It is important to remember that communication is more about active listening and engaging with the other person than expressing your own point of view. It's about relating to and building bridges with one another. Eye contact, body language and listening to the other person are an important part of this process. It's less about the words or content of your talk. It's your body language (such as responsive tone, facial expression and mirroring of the other person) that builds rapport.

When you listen to other people and understand their needs, you can influence them easily. For creating genuine human connection, you need to develop the skill of listening to others, understanding their needs and concerns and appreciating them. These show them that you are sincere. While dealing with others, you should make them look good, feel valued and put them at the center of your attention. By doing so, you will create trust and a personal bond. Irrespective of your future business engagement or not, you will build a rapport with that person. You can use this relationship for other constructive purposes too. We are living in a digital age right now. As people are bombarded with information, they have a smaller attention span. They hardly follow what others say. If you develop a habit of listening to others, it will make you unique among the crowd. As people have two ears and one mouth, you should listen more and talk less. It will make you a more attractive person. It will also help you to build personal connections which is a key element of leadership skills.

BE EMPATHETIC TO OTHERS

As people are preoccupied with social media newsfeeds nowadays, they have less time for each other. People are becoming more and more self-centered. We have insights into this trend when we see selfie madness and thoughtless photo and video sharing of people on social media. In the pre-digital age, people would help one another in accidents and disaster situations. Nowadays, instead of helping out people whose lives are in grave danger, many opt for taking selfies or videos of human disasters. A large section of people remains so drowned in social media that they have little time or interest in meeting people in real life. It's becoming a new kind of addiction. As a result, people are increasingly losing touch with and empathy for each other. As empathy is increasingly becoming a scarce resource, people who possess it will be in high demand. An average person nowadays doesn't reflect or look within to find out their own limitations in order to take corrective action. They prefer to point their fingers at others as if they are to blame for their limitations. This manifests in short-sightedness and narrow-mindedness. Nowadays, social media platforms are also used for spreading propaganda, gossip and rumors. Sometimes, they are used as tool for inciting violence. As a result of such abuse, community cohesion suffers.

For success, you must hold yourself accountable for all your thoughts, actions and inactions. You must also cultivate empathy, love and respect for others. You should keep in mind that it's not only you but all people who have their own struggles, hopes and dreams. In order to become empathetic, you should be non-judgmental, kind and supportive to others. This will help you to better understand other people's needs and the underlying causes of their actions and behaviors. Those insights will give you inner confidence in dealing with others. By being empathetic, you will develop better interpersonal communication skills. You can profitably use this to improve your personal and professional life. Showing sincere interest and empathy towards others will make you a more approachable and likeable person. It will help you to manage interpersonal relationships in a better way. In workplaces, there are personality conflicts and clashes that lower the overall productivity of organizations. As some people are not empathetic, they easily become critical and even aggressive towards others. When you practice empathy, other people will open up to you. This will enable you to reach out and avoid unnecessary conflicts in a work environment. Developing empathy will make you a better person, as well as help you to advance professionally.

BE HONORABLE

Honor is a higher order need of individuals: it motivates people to act for a higher purpose than themselves. Because of this, people can expand their circle of empathy from their close family members to community, nation and the world. A vast majority of people in the world struggle to fulfill their primary needs – they get less opportunities for fulfilling higher needs. Only after filling primary needs, can people attempt to fulfill their need for honor and self-actualization, which are way higher needs for them. To become a person of character and value, you have to become honorable in the first place. When you reach this state, you cannot take advantage or be unjust to others. An honorable person lives a life based on principles, not on personal convenience or gain. This builds up an internal parameter that forces people to uphold their standards when dealing with others. When you attach value to your personal identity and reputation, you put your credibility over and above everything else. No matter how seductive it may seem, you cannot take the low road. If someone treats you unfairly by stooping low, don't do the same. Rather, you take the high road.

To live an honorable life, first of all, you must perceive yourself as an honorable person. You will also need to treat people with honesty, respect and empathy. This will help others to trust you. Indian Sanskrit epic, Mahabharata, tells the story of the honorable spirit of the Pandava princes and their heroic fights against their cousin, Kauravas, to uphold their principles. One of the key takeaways from the epic is: you have to stand up for what is right and even fight to uphold principles, if necessary. Remember, an honorable person will not employ the wrong means to achieve goals. By following an honorable path, you can build a solid reputation. This will separate you from the crowd. It's the path of heroes and heroines.

IMPROVE COMMUNICATION SKILLS

Communication skills are some of the most important skills for career and life success. We often see paradoxes in relation to this. On the one hand, there are highly-qualified people who cannot fulfill their true potential due to their poor communication skills. On the other hand, we see people with less knowledge and professional skills who get promoted to managerial and leadership positions due to their superior communication skills. Here, communication skills make a difference. The latter group is good at articulating their thoughts as concrete points and communicating these through good presentations. It's a highly-valued skill that you should master. For achieving rapid career, business or life success, you must improve your communication skills. Speech gives you a powerful tool at your disposal which will help you to present your thoughts concretely, persuade people and improve your chances of success. It can open a new world of opportunities for you.

Roman statesman, orator, lawyer and philosopher Marcus Tullius Cicero, in addition to great speakers of the modern era, (such as Winston Churchill, John F. Kennedy, Martin Luther King Jr., and Seikh Mujibur Rahman) rose to prominence by combining political vision with the power of speech. Churchill's "I have nothing to offer but blood, toil, tears and sweat", Kennedy's "Ask not what your country can do for you, ask what you can do for your country", and King's "I have a dream" are all lines taken from speeches that have inspired millions of people worldwide.

THE POWER OF A SPEECH

Seikh Mujibur Rahman, the founding father of Bangladesh and also known as *Bangabandhu* (Friend of Bengal), inspired the historically-suppressed Bengali nation under foreign rule to independence. A true democrat and a man of his people, he embraced long-term imprisonments during Pakistani rule. He inspired the dream of the Bengali people to fight for their own rights from Pakistani rule through his 7 March 1971 speech, "This time the struggle is for our freedom. This time the struggle is for our independence." The historic speech that called for the liberation of Bengali people from Pakistan, in front of hundreds of thousands of people in Dhaka, has been included by UNESCO as a *documentary heritage of the world*. Rahman led Bangladesh to independence on 16 December 1971 after nine months of guerilla warfare against the powerful Pakistani army with the support of India. According to a BBC poll, he is considered the greatest Bengali in the nation's history over the past thousand years.

Words are less important in interpersonal communications than one may think. It is not what you say but how you say it, that is important. Your body language and tone of voice are much more important than the message you deliver with words. Keeping those in mind, you should develop your communication skills. For successful communication, you also need to understand what motivates your audience. Most people feel that they are the center of the universe and act in self-centered ways. This approach does not inspire interest and confidence in others. You have to develop skills in understanding or reading people (i.e. recognizing the true person beneath their social mask). When you can develop this emotional intelligence, you will be able to understand people better and react and communicate with them in more appropriate ways. These people-reading skills, together with communication skills, will make you way smarter. You have to use every social opportunity to polish your communication skills.

ALWAYS STAY PREPARED

When you are going to meet a person or deliver a message at an event, you must do your homework beforehand. Before a meeting, you should clearly set an agenda so that you can put forward your points to the other side. If you are going to present a paper in a seminar or conference, you should prepare your presentation and practice it before the formal presentation itself. Preparation is the key to effective communication. If you are going to have a job interview over the telephone, write down the answers to potential questions as well as your own questions. Once you do your homework by practicing, you can be precise in putting your points across. You must have noticed that stage performers perform very well in front of a large audience without suffering from stage fright. How do they do it? Don't you think you can do the same? Yes, you can. As the audience, we see the performance of such people but not their behind-the-curtains preparations for the final act. Even professional performers spend hours preparing for an event.

Adequate preparation will make you appear natural to others in professional as well as personal settings. This will give you the opportunity to ensure your presence is felt in meetings or events. It will remove fear from your mind and make you more confident. So, embrace preparation. When preparation meets opportunity, people call this success. Once you are properly prepared, you can convey your message better. It also motivates you to volunteer in different roles within your organization. Most people who are employees are after job security only and are not ready to push beyond their defined roles within an organization. When you can voluntarily take on additional responsibilities, you will attract the attention of your manager or boss. This will unveil new opportunities for you. When your preparation meets with the right opportunities, you will prove your skills. As a result, you will get promoted in your career much faster than others.

BE AN UNFORGETTABLE PERSON

If you want to become successful, you must dream, dress, act and live as successful people do. You should demand higher standards from yourself. It's important that you develop professional knowledge, as well as good communication skills. Keep in mind one important thing. In this visual world, average people cannot see your inner substance. They will treat you according to your outer appearance.

During our school years in Bangladesh, we heard a popular tale of Persian poet Seikh Saadi who is also known as Saadi Sirazi. On the way to visit the King's palace, Seikh Saadi went to spend a night in the house of a nobleman. Seeing his ordinary dress, the nobleman did not show Saadi honor and hospitality. In the King's palace, he received honor and gorgeous clothes as a gift. On his way back, Saadi took shelter in the same nobleman's house in his gorgeous outfit. This time, his host received him with respect and entertained him with rich and delicious foods. To the host's surprise, Saadi started putting the foods in the pockets of his clothes. When asked about his strange behavior, he replied that it was not him but his clothing that deserved the treat.

It is very important that you treat people with dignity irrespective of their money or class. However, it is also important that you dress appropriately so that people don't undermine you. To become successful, you must work, act and dress like successful people do. As everybody won't have any idea about your inner qualities, it is important for you to dress like a decent person. Don't compromise on this. People naturally want to get along with smart, rich and successful people. Your appearance, gestures, inner substance, outlook and communication skills should reflect that you are a resourceful person. Sometimes, in order to build credibility, you must show the depth of your skills to others. There is nothing wrong with this. In order to keep your edge, you must develop people skills in addition to your professional knowledge, skills and expertise. The combination of all these skills will build your personal brand as an unforgettable person.

BUILD YOUR NETWORK

Personal development is an individual process. By following this path, you can prepare yourself for taking on greater challenges in life. However, you cannot create a highly successful and meaningful life by this alone. For greater success, you will need to connect with others to build up your network. By serving others, you can deepen your impact sand build a rewarding life. You should use every opportunity to expand your social circles so that you can have maximum impact on others' lives. In the real world, recruitment is done through personal contacts i.e. on a "who knows who" basis. Nobody wants to hire a complete stranger or untested person in any organization. Organizations are constantly seeking employees with the right attitude, professional knowledge and communication skills. Expanding your network will not only help you get a job, but will also help you to get promoted. By following this path, you can also become an entrepreneur. Your professional and personal network will help you by creating a strong foundation for your success. You can use membership in voluntary organizations and alumni associations, as well as participation in conferences and seminars, as platforms for building your professional network.

CREATE A PERSONAL LEGACY

The human lifespan is relatively short. Within this short life, people try to fulfill their primary as well as higher needs of life. A vast majority of people in the world struggle to fill their primary needs. Fulfilling higher needs such as honor and self-actualization are far beyond their reach. You can move in that direction through becoming successful in your career. It is true that you can be successful by attaining individual pursuits. However, true success lies in serving others and creating significance in your life. Whatever station of life you are in, you can always serve others. It does not even require money. Treating others with gentleness, kindness and love can create a culture of peace in the world. Human life on the earth is quite short. In every seventy years or so, a generation of people disappears from earth. Soon after their death, the memories of most of them fade away from people's minds. Most of their bodies are laid in unmarked graves. Those who are lucky get tombstones on their graves. Only a tiny section of them live in people's hearts long after their death due to their selfless contribution to others. They become legends in the public imagination. Only through serving others, can you create your own personal significance and legacy. People will remember you for your contributions to society and the broader world. Alfred Nobel, the creator of the Nobel Prize, died over a century ago. But his noble legacy continues to inspire people of the world to undertake extraordinary service for the peace and progress of the humanity. Following the example of such a great soul, as well as others, you can create your own legacy. Whether the deed is big or small, it doesn't matter. It's spirit that matters.

It is a fact that self-preservation and preservation of one's family members are primary reasons why people toil in this world. Besides serving the needs of yourself and your family, you should also extend this empathy to others in the community. You should understand that other people are also going through their own problems and struggling to make sense of their lives amidst chaos. Try to understand their needs and if possible, try to help them fulfill their positive aspirations. Only through your contribution in uplifting others, can you create your own significance in this world. As a person, you should possess qualities such as patience, optimism, trust, competence and reliability. Inside and outside, you should build up a balanced personality that people trust and turn to, if necessary. Your positive qualities will make you stand out among the crowd. This should work as your personal brand. When people hear your name, they should get the sense of a person with valuable skills, competence, reliability and compassion for others. Whatever you do, you should keep in mind that you are representing yourself to the world. You should fiercely protect your reputation. This should be reflected in every action you take. Not only should you pursue success, you should also support and inspire others to success. It will make you a natural leader in professional life as well as in family, community life and beyond. A life with a broader purpose will make you a truly successful, distinct and fulfilled person. By pursuing this path, you will live a life of true adventure.

SELF-ASSESSMENT/ACTIONS

List the top three things you want to be remembered for after your death.

1. ____

2. ____

3. ____

List three top people skills that will make you a remarkable person.

1. ____

2. ____

3. ____

List timeframes for achieving three people skills.

1. ____

2. ____

3. ____

Skill one: list three specific actions to acquire this skill.

1. ____

2. ____

3. ____

Skill two: list three specific actions to acquire this skill.

1. ____

2. ____

3. ____

Skill three: list three specific actions to acquire this skill.

1. ____

2. ____

3. ____

CHAPTER 9

TAKE THE THREE-MONTH CHALLENGE

By following old and new Eastern and Western wisdom, as well as the easy-to-follow formula of this book, you will be able to change your career and life thoroughly. It will help you to discover your passion, identify individual talents, make a tailored career plan and take action to achieve massive career success. As you align your career goals with broader life goals, you will be able to reach your goals faster. It is important that you regularly track your progress. As said earlier, you must take control of your time to implement your career development plan. Implemented correctly, this will surely transform your life. It will tremendously increase your value in the marketplace and take your career to a new height. It's a self-directed conscious path that will boost your confidence to a new level. It will increase your effectiveness and make you irreplaceable in your career. You will be able to create a personal brand that represents knowledge, skills and integrity. You will become a valuable and resourceful person. You will be rewarded with money, social recognition, leadership and fame. If you can put your skills into entrepreneurship, you can become one of the next billionaires. Only you can decide how far you want to go. There is no limit to this success.

On the way to career success, you will face many hurdles. As it is impossible to achieve a larger goal overnight, you must divide your long-term goal into specific and actionable short-term goals. At the end of each chapter, you will find a personal assessment/actions section that will help you to find your passion, discover your strengths, set up goals and ways to implement these. Keeping in mind your long-term goals, you should start implementing your short-term goals. You must follow daily discipline to reach your weekly, monthly and yearly goals. It's about acquiring new skills through developing new habits, as well as retaining and strengthening these. Once you achieve a goal, you should celebrate it. Then, you can move on to the next. Keep in mind that, primarily, you are the sole author of your life. You cannot depend on others to write your script. That's why you must become your own truest friend. If you don't remain loyal to your own career and life goals, who else can do you this favour? As a sudden break of discipline can derail you from achieving your goals, it is important that you keep moving with your goals no matter what. If for some reason it does not work, you need to adjust your tactics to fit with circumstances.

As habits are the key differentiator between a successful and an average person, it is highly important that you start developing success habits. For developing new habits, you must to go beyond your comfort zone and practice every day for the maximum possible number of hours. You have to focus on one thing at a time with full concentration. As described earlier, when repetition of action is carried out on a consistent basis over a long period of time, a habit becomes natural or automatic. It's time for you to take the first challenge of acquiring a new success habit. A three-month period is enough time for making your first breakthrough in building a new habit. With initial success, you will be motivated to work on this further. With investment of additional time and resources, you can deepen this habit. When you develop and consolidate one habit, you can go for the next. You can continue this process for six months, one year, two years, five years or even ten years. It will take your skills to new heights. You can become a world-class performer in your niche. When you do so, you will become unstoppable in your career. You will attract success like a magnet. This will work as an insurance for you against career uncertainties. You can achieve as much success as you want. The sky is not the limit.

Life by its very nature is uncertain. In this age of automation and artificial intelligence, certain old professions are becoming obsolete and new professions are emerging. If, for some reasons beyond your control, you become out of your work or business, the lessons of this book will help you to make a strong comeback. You will be able thrive again in your chosen course with a new momentum. You can be more successful than ever before. You will prove your critics wrong. With a new mindset, career plan and actions, you will achieve massive career success.

If you follow my guidance, I can guarantee that you will rock both in career and life. Initially, I urge you to take a three-month career challenge of acquiring a new habit for skill development. You can do it. In fact, anybody can do it. The initial victory will drive you to take more and more action. After success in the initial three-month challenge, you must consolidate your gains. You must go for implementing six-month, one-year, three-year, five-year and even ten-year challenges. Within three to five years, you will create massive career success. In ten years, you will become a world-class professional. You will be a highly-successful person with effectiveness, happiness, meaning and fulfillment in life. Your life will be a true adventure. Through your deeds, you can become a beacon of hope for the world. You too can make history. I wish you the best of luck. Go ahead with this non-violent personal revolution! Achieve massive career success! Improve yourself to change the world!

SELF-ASSESSMENT/ACTIONS

List three top skills that will advance your career significantly.

1. ____

2. ____

3. ____

For achieving your No.1 skill, what habits must you develop?

1. ____

2. ____

3. ____

For achieving your No.1 habit, what actions must you undertake?

1. ____

2. ____

3. ____

For developing your No.1 habit, what single action must you take daily for three months?

1. ____

2. ____

3. ____

Specify daily, weekly and monthly allocation of hours for practice with a concrete routine.

1. ____

2. ____

3. ____

ABOUT THE AUTHOR

Mojibur Doftori is an expert on international education, career skills, business, leadership development and life success. He has more than twenty-five years of experience as a journalist, researcher, university teacher and expert on global governance issues, with experience in Asia, Europe and Africa.

A thought leader and speaker, he also worked as a researcher at PEN International headquarters in London. He lives in Helsinki, Finland.